STRING ART
magic

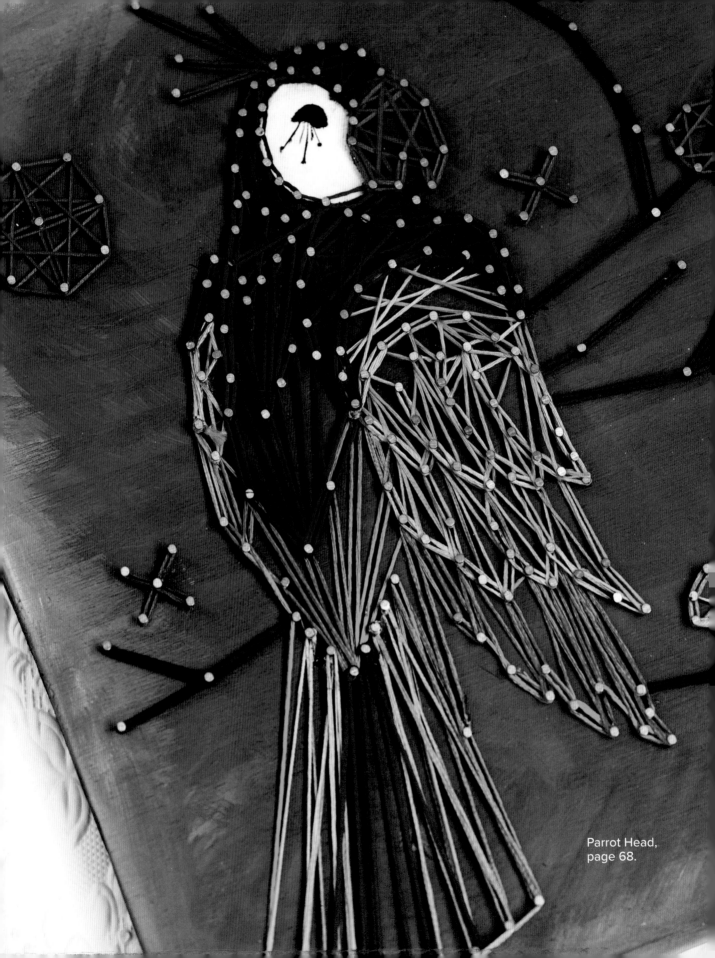

Parrot Head,
page 68.

STRING ART
magic

The Secrets to Crafting
Geometric Art with String & Nail

Rain Blanken

SPRING HOUSE PRESS

Publisher: Paul McGahren
Editorial Director: Matthew Teague
Editor: Kerri Grzybicki
Design: Lindsay Hess
Layout: Jodie Delohery
Photography: Danielle Atkins

Spring House Press
P.O. Box 239
Whites Creek, TN 37189

ISBN: 978-1-940611-73-0

Library of Congress Control Number: 2018938701

Printed in the United States of America

10 9 8 7 6 5 4 3 2 1

Note: The following list contains names used in *String Art Magic* that may be registered with the United States Copyright Office: *Aladdin*; *Alice in Wonderland*; *Annie* ("Tomorrow"); *Beauty and the Beast*; Beatles ("Here Comes the Sun"); Bill Withers ("Ain't No Sunshine"); Cheshire Cat; Etsy; George Boole; George Everest; Google; *Hoarders*; Instagram; John Eichinger; Kings Island (The Beast); Lois Kreischer; MacArthur Award; MacGyver; Mark Jansen; M&Ms; Nick Offerman; Nobel Prize; Open Door Enterprises; Pierre Bézier; *Pinocchio*; Ric Barline; *Sailor Moon; Scooby Doo*; *String Art Symmography, Three-Dimensional Creative Designs with Yarn without Knotting or Knitting*; Super Mario Bros 3; *The Art of Thread Design*; *The Preparation of the Child for Science*; Tiny Tim; Queen's College; Walt Disney; "You Are My Sunshine."

To learn more about Spring House Press books, or to find a retailer near you, email info@springhousepress.com or visit us at www.springhousepress.com.

Rainbow Mandala, page 34.

CONTENTS

But First . . . Coffee

State Scrapbook

Ahoy Matey

Rainbow Mandala

Sugar Skull

Evening Star

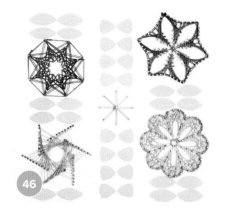

Swedish Blooms

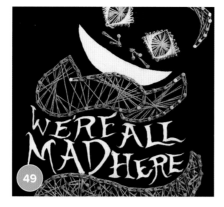

Vanishing Cheshire Cat

Lucky Butterfly

Which Way to the Beach?

Here Comes the Sun

Tropical Kiss

Parrot Head

Octopus's Garden

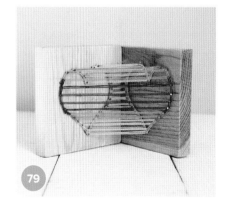

3-D Hearts

INTRODUCTION

I first tried my hand at string art in 1993. I think.

Those awkward pre-teen years in the late '90s all tend to blend together. For me it was a lot of awkward exchanges and waking up at 7 a.m. to record *Sailor Moon* on VHS. I lived with my three sisters, mom, and grandma just north of Dayton, Ohio. It was a small township that consisted mostly of cornfields and cows with big tags clamped onto their ears that I still suspect indicated their doom. There wasn't a whole lot to do out there, so I spent my time exploring the house. My grandma collected rooms full of unused merchandise before *Hoarders* made it cool.

One day while swimming through the back porch, I discovered a small white box with a parrot on the front. The string art kit was one of many manufactured by Open Door Enterprises, a company that saw a solid financial opportunity in the string art craze of the 1970s. It was designed by John Eichinger, one of the most prolific mid-century thread artists.

But 13-year-old me didn't care about any of that. This box looked like something to do during a summer when my best friend Tiffany was busy a lot with her family. Also, her number had some zeros in it and those took forever to dial on a rotary phone.

I didn't know what I was doing when I started my first string art project, which tells me now that you really don't need much to get started. The kit came with string, pins, a corkboard, and some *lovely* black felt. I would later learn that black felt was integral to the structure of all string art in the '70s.

With the help of the pattern, I was able to create a very intricate parrot design with my dumb little hands, probably pushing my giant glasses up my nose and periodically wiping the sweat underneath my *Aladdin* ballcap. If that hopeless nerd can do it, so can you.

Why a Book on Geometric String Art?

After that first flirtation with string art as a kid, I took a 20-year hiatus. The main reason? Beyond the old box I found at grandma's, the world didn't have a lot to offer a budding string artist. The "thread art" of the 1970s was a fad—just like macramé. And just like macramé, it only lived in dusty pamphlets and out-of-print books. A lot of the patterns I could find were dark depictions of sailboats and the same glaring owls.

String art in all forms disappeared from the 1980s 'til about 2010. Then, it re-emerged in a boom as creations of nails, wood, and randomly wound string that colored in simple shapes and names. I was excited to see some incarnation of the craft I'd tried as a kid, but had known string art to be something entirely different. The new designs were a far cry from the pin-by-pin

instructions that I followed religiously to create my funkadelic parrot.

The new freeform string art designs felt a bit like coloring within the lines. They were cool in their own way, but I felt like I was in a bizarro craft universe where those beautiful geometric designs from the '70s never existed.

I wanted to help revive the old geometric style and blend the new with the old. I liked making freeform string art, but my geometric roots wanted something more intricate. But I couldn't find any geometric string art books published past the early 1980s. None.

Upon further Internet searching, I found that geometric string art was all but dead. New string artists are budding on Instagram, displaying the same intricate geometric shapes that I admired as a kid. Across social media, we trade tips on the craft and demonstrate technique.

So, in *String Art Magic,* I'm applying the repeating parabolic angles that created the stoic pin-and-felt '70s designs while working in the bolder and brighter techniques from modern freeform string art.

I also wanted to tell the story of the origins of string art, namely the contributions of a trailblazing feminist you've probably never heard of: Mary Everest Boole. If Claude Monet was the father of Impressionism, Mary Everest Boole was the mother of geometric string art. I contacted her family for an exclusive look at her life, including a never-before-published photo of Mary for the book (because that one you may have seen on the Internet is gettin' pretty tired).

In addition to following the projects step by step, I encourage you to eventually go rogue and apply the project lessons to your own original creations. Note that each project in *String Art Magic* has been purposefully designed to teach a lesson. Here's a freebie: Don't hit your fingers with the hammer. Read on for additional gems.

A BRIEF HISTORY OF STRING ART

Mary Everest Boole: Our Lady Madonna of String Art or "Mother Mary"

Who invented sewing? Batik dying? Printmaking? Even if we had a time machine and knew where to look, most art forms have evolved slowly over time, with many hands weaving the tapestry of human culture. For string artists of the geometric variety, though, we are fortunate to be able to pinpoint the founder of our work: Mary Everest Boole.

During the Victorian era of England, Mary was an author, feminist philosopher, and mathematician who invented the geometric string art methods to which you'll completely dedicate your life after reading this book. She advocated for women to be taken seriously intellectually, and practiced progressive teaching methods that connected math with everyday application.

Mary Everest Boole worked as a librarian at Queen's College in London while tutoring on the side to circumvent a silly 1800s rule that prohibited female teachers at universities. She raised five daughters on her own, all of whom grew up to be successful; some famous. Mary was a math master, an author, and a quirky rebel.

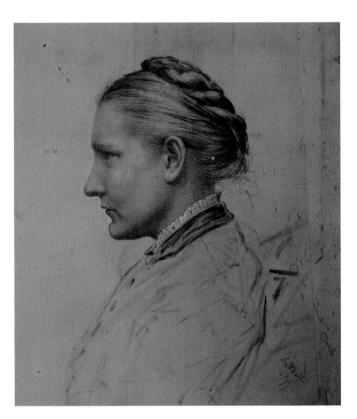

WHO WAS MARY?

Mary's story can be found in the corners of the Internet, mired in remnants of middle-school geometry class assignments. She is often overlooked, most likely due to the fame of her husband, mathematician George Boole, and uncle, George Everest (as in Mount Everest). The Georges influenced and supported Mary's education in math and science, but we'll stop with them there. As a wife/niece who is also an independent human/successful woman, I'd be miffed if the first line of my biography always started with who my husband and uncle were.

Little is publicly known about Mary, so I reached out to her great-great-granddaughter, Marni Rosner. Marni described Mary as "a brilliant eccentric who was ahead of her time," and spoke of Mary's tireless advocacy to teach math to girls in the Victorian era.

Marni commented, "[She was] a penniless widow with five daughters to raise, [which] would be overwhelming, even today. That she managed to think, learn, write, publish, [and] carry on such a complex intellectual life in the mid-nineteenth century is nothing short of amazing.

"Her correspondence with Hebrew scholars and exploration of East Indian weaving and embroidery patterns reveal the intellectual freedom of a seeking, open mind. [She] refused to be daunted by poverty, [and] child care responsibilities . . . Imagine if she had been able to attend a university herself and had access to today's educational facilities."

MARY'S PATIENCE WITH THOSE WHO STINK AT MATH

My math skills are akin to my running ability—used sparingly, and only when I'm trying to get away (e.g., bears, the IRS, or struggling to leave a lunch tip). Yes, that's right, I'm piloting this geometric ship you're on, and I'm mathematically impaired. Sure, I can add up my bills, but only thanks to whatever magic is stuffed inside a calculator. If you run or do math well, you are a demigod in my eyes.

Mary Everest Boole understood the struggle of math dum-dums like me. She recognized that math needed to be made fun, and that her students, especially young girls, often lost interest in math at an early age due to the dry way in which it was taught.

Mary once wrote, "The cultivation of the mathematical imagination should include not only its development but its orderly and systematic exercise." She was a big believer in working creativity and story into learning mathematics, commenting that "We use the imagination as freely as the hands and eyes." She was not satisfied with common teaching practices that detached math from natural discovery and application, and believed that without making math interactive, the student would not retain it.

Indeed, in ye olde 1980s, I was busy drawing ponies on math worksheets. I cannot remember a single math class in which I was excited (unless the lesson involved subtracting M&Ms). I would probably have been better off a hundred years ago with Mary, and my experience is not unique.

MARY'S CLEVER DISCOVERY

To make math relatable to young girls, Mary developed a method of using sewing cards to demonstrate how straight lines could be organized to create curved shapes. The craft of working with string and paper effectively engaged students in the lesson.

In her 1904 publication, *The Preparation of the Child for Science*, Mary recounted her string art discovery: "In my young days, cards of different shapes were sold in pairs, in fancy shops, for making needle-books and pin-cushions. The cards were intended to be painted on; and there was a row of holes round the edge by which twin cards were to be sewn together . . . I can feel now the delight with which I discovered that the little blank space so left in the middle of the card was bounded by a symmetrical curve made up of a tiny bit of each of my straight silk lines . . . As the practical art of sewing perforated card was already quite familiar to me, my brain was free to receive as a

seed the discovery I had made . . . all the more because no one spoke to me then of tangents."

More than 100 years later, the lesson resonates with Marni. She says of Mary's writing, "[It] explained that women used math, particularly geometry and spatial reasoning, all the time in their intricate lace, weaving, [and] knitting patterns, which most women of her day kept in their heads. She believed that girls should first be praised for these skills, and then be taught to build upon this spatial reasoning in the teaching of mathematics."

MARY IN THE MODERN AGE

In the present, it can be difficult to imagine the frustrations that Mary Everest Boole faced in her mission to make math fun. I asked Marni if she thought Mary's career and resulting notoriety would have been different if she had been a present-day educator.

Marni replied with pride, "Yes, I imagine today she would be heading an entire research department and would be receiving MacArthur Awards or a Nobel Prize . . . she was a moral voice generations ahead of her time; condemning religious and race prejudice at a time when both were completely acceptable in Ireland and England."

I may never be good at math, but Mary's lessons on spatial reasoning at least lit up the part of my brain that handles parabolic angles. I adore my knowledge of angles and measurements and the ability to create something beautiful. Suddenly, math became a useful tool for me instead of a terrible chore.

String art has evolved since Mary's cards and silk thread, but her ideas and enthusiasm will live on if we value a creative approach to all aspects of education. It is my mission that Mary's efforts will not be lost to history. Let's say it loud and say it often: "Thanks, Mary!"

String Art in the '70s

Geometric string art hit a boom in the 1970s, when people clamored to offset their wood-paneled walls with every fabric craft imaginable. String art patterns flowed through the craft aisles right alongside macramé owls and crocheted curtains.

This can probably be attributed to the publicity of the Bézier curve in 1962. This instrument of arithmetic was introduced by Pierre Bézier, a French mathematician and engineer. He used the term to describe a curve that passes through at least four points: the beginning point, the ending point, and at least two points in between. Adjusting the points in between changes the shape of the curve. It was all the rage in

"70s Throwback Owl" by Linsey Dryden, *@lsd_stringart*

"Abstract Flower" by Linsey Dryden, *@lsd_stringart*

computer applications and inspired many string artists during the mid-century.

DIY books and kits fueled the string art fad through the '60s and '70s. Open Door Enterprises, founded in 1969 by Ric Barline and Mark Jansen, created a popular line of string art kits. These included a colorful parrot, the first string art project I ever took on—after finding it in my grandma's stuff in the '90s! (I'm not that old, jeez—and see page 8.)

Pioneering string artist John Eichinger provided many geometric designs for the Open Door kits, and is often credited with coining the term "string mandala" to describe circular designs. 1974's *The Art of Thread Design* was a handy reference for plotting circular designs, in which Mark Jansen oddly tried to copyright the ancient Hindu word "mandala." Jansen's book also featured lots of black felt, which I don't recommend unless you're trying to complement an orange shag rug.

If you've looked up classic geometric string art books, chances are you've seen the owl on the cover of Lois Kreischer's 1971 publication bearing the curiously long name *String Art Symmography, Three-Dimensional Creative Designs with Yarn without Knotting or Knitting*. The bright oranges and greens of Lois's work are decidedly early '70s in style, but the patterns are solid.

Modern String Art

After the '70s, the popularity of geometric string art all but died out. But the bloom of Etsy shops and Instagram accounts has sparked a renewed interest in string crafts. "Freeform" string art does not follow a strict pattern of angles and plot points as geometric string art does, but instead relies on randomly (yet strategically) filling in an outline with string to create a design.

Freeform string art seems to have permeated every festival, craft show, and

"String Art Camper" by Kelly O'Bryant, *@my2heartstrings*

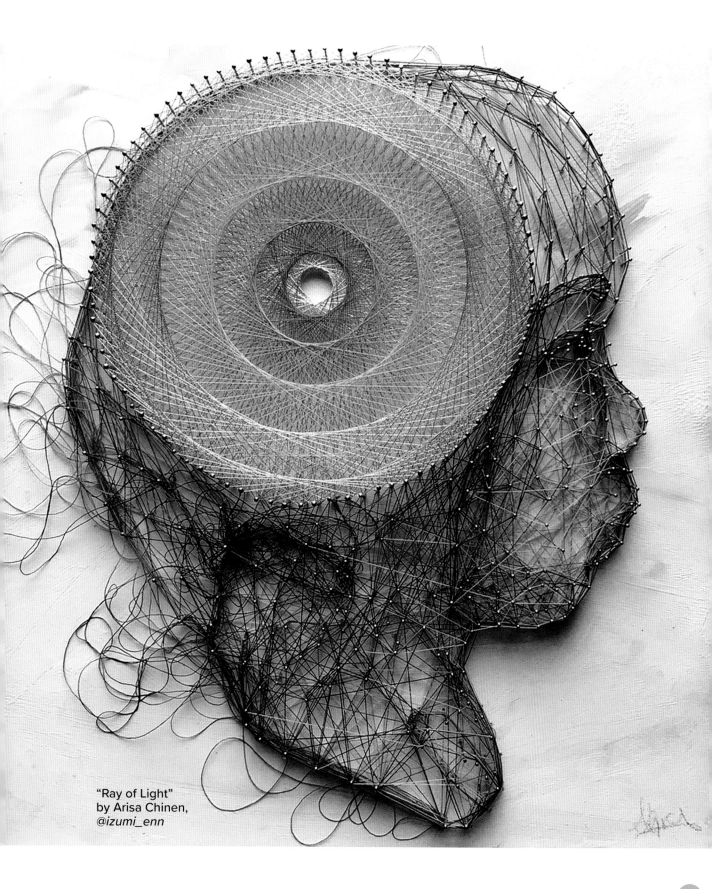

"Ray of Light"
by Arisa Chinen,
@izumi_enn

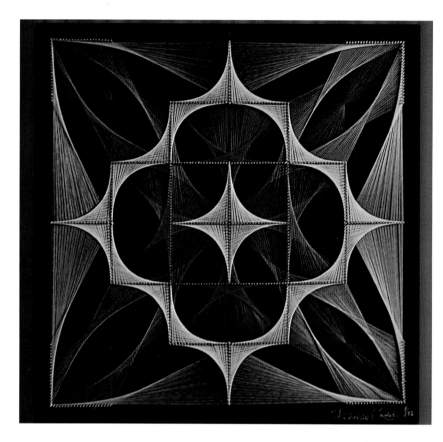

"Marilyn Monroe V2.0"
by Christopher Panic Love,
@*deviant.twine*
(opposite page)

By Fabricio Carlos Pereira,
@*fabricio_artista* (left)

"The Leather Elephant"
by Thomas Lanceleur,
@*stringartbytom* (below)

Etsy shop. A quick jaunt on the Internet will reveal standard freeform designs such as states, baby elephants, and wedding dates.

Creating your own freeform pattern is quite simple. Unlike geometric string art, all you need is the outline of a shape on wood and the will to go to town on it with nails and string. Unfortunately, this means that clever freeform designs created by independent artists have been duplicated so many times that it can be difficult to pinpoint who originated the design. Often-duplicated designs include a strung mason jar filled with silk flowers, or Kelly O'Bryant's original camper design, pictured on page 14.

"Merry Bulbs"
((left) and "You Are
Loved" (below) by
Lauren Honaker,
@thehonakerhome

By Fabricio
Carlos Pereira,
@fabricio_artista
(bottom right)

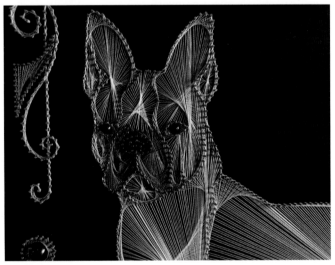

Freeform string art brings a handmade, rustic element into our modernized homes. It's the pop art equivalent of the classic geometric pieces. Straightforward imagery makes the complexity of geometric string art unnecessary for the success of the design. However, I'm here to show you that geometric string art isn't all that complicated, and just as enjoyable!

SUPPLIES

Nails, Nails, Nails

Nails are very important because they form the anchor points for the string in creating each pattern. I prefer to work with ½-inch nails in my string art, so that's what you'll be using. (When you write a book, you can use whatever nails you like.) ½-inch nails are long enough to hold the thread, but don't take more than a couple whacks with a hammer to sink.

Every string artist needs a trusty hammer. Nothing heavy duty is required here; be advised that a large, heavy hammer can quickly give you sore arm muscles. Go small. Even a small ball-peen hammer is enough to do the job.

Some projects also include ¾-inch wire brads. Brads are like nails, but skinnier and with tiny heads. These are great for minimalizing the appearance of nails in your work, or for designs that require points that are very close together.

There are also a few mentions of 1-inch nails. Long nails are used when a lot of thread is required to fit on the nail, or to add dimension to the piece. For example, in my take on the enchanted rose from *Beauty and the Beast* above, the nails creating the glass jar are longer than the brads used for the rose, allowing the strings forming the glass to overlap those of the rose.

String

The string is what will form your designs. What you use for string is totally up to you. I enjoy working with embroidery thread because it comes in absolutely every color imaginable (even glittery ones) and is cheap. String artists work with embroidery thread, nylon string, jute twine, ribbon, copper wire, or whatever grabs their attention. As you work through the projects in this book, I encourage you to experiment with various string media.

Suddenly Woodworking

You'll need a plank or block of wood to serve as your canvas. I wasn't in the habit of cutting and sanding wood before I started creating string art. Turns out, it's not that tough, and can be quite the Zen experience. I'm still no Nick Offerman, but I've bungled my way into acquiring a few woodworking skills.

Softwoods are your most likely candidates for a string art canvas. As the name indicates, softwoods are easier to work with than hardwoods. By nail #127, you'll thank me. Softwoods include pine, cedar, yew, Douglas fir, spruce, and redwood. Yellow birch, northern red oak, and cherry are hardwoods that aren't too hard to work with, either. Look up the Janka hardness test for a handy scale of softer to harder woods.

Blocks and sheets of softwood are easy to find at hardware stores, and there are even pre-cut decorative pieces at craft stores. Pine tends to be the cheapest and easiest to find. All projects in this book require boards at least ¾-inch thick.

Use coarse 60- to 80-grit sandpaper to slough off all the nasty splinter hopefuls from the edges and smooth out any rough spots on the front. The board is an integral part of the artwork, so address it as such. I've painted, stained, or decoupaged the boards in the following projects, but I encourage you to experiment with your own styles of board treatment. In the '70s, for example, it was very popular to cover the boards in fabric. They used a lot of velvet and felt, as everyone did in the '70s at any opportunity, but you can use cotton, linen, muslin, or even a potato sack for a rustic look.

Hangers

There are plenty of ways to affix hardware to the back of your board, but I prefer sawtooth hangers. They will come with two tiny nails to keep them in place, and are easy to adjust and straighten on the wall.

OVERVIEW OF THE PROCESS

Prepare the Pattern

Mom taught us not to rip pages out of books, but in this case, it's okay. The patterns at 100% size in this book can be reused if you're careful, but I recommend making copies. See below for large pattern assembly instructions. You are welcome to shrink patterns, but keep in mind that the nails may be too close together.

After the board is prepped per project instructions, cut away all extra paper around the numbers and dots on the pattern. Position the pattern as you like (typically centered) on the board. Tape in a few spots to hold in place.

LARGE PATTERN ASSEMBLY INSTRUCTIONS

Some of my patterns span pages or are too large for 8 ½ x 11-inch copy paper; just too much awesome to fit! Creativity should never be limited by size. I've added crosshairs to these patterns to help with assembly.

For patterns at 100%, carefully tear out the patterns, or to spare your precious book, copy sections of the pattern as needed to fit onto 8 ½ x 11-inch paper. You already bought the book, so do whatever you want with it (except use pages as toilet paper; that's just rude). Patterns that

need enlarged should be copied at the percentage shown.

Trim around pattern pieces and cut alongside the crosshairs. Position pieces on a window, or even a bright TV or computer monitor. Align crosshairs and tape the pattern pieces together.

Pattern Elements

- Dots on each pattern are representative of where nails will be placed on the design. Where smaller dots appear, this indicates using a smaller nail or wire brad.
- Numbers on each pattern may not mark every nail and will typically not be strung entirely in numerical sequence. Follow the instructions closely, as the pattern may jump from nail #1 to nail #88.
- Blocks of color on patterns are indicative of painted or freeform-filled areas.

Adding Nails

Moving forward, choose how you'd like to use the pattern to nail and string:

- **Newbie's Delight:** Drive nails through a copy of the pattern, then string the design. This can work out well for kids or those who are new to stringing and may need to follow the string lines on the pattern. The downside is that it can be difficult to rip the pattern from underneath the string, and the pattern copy inevitably gets ruined.

- **Training Wheels:** Drive nails through the pattern, but remove it before stringing. This option makes sure each dot has a nail, but you'll need to carefully pop the pattern off each nail head to keep the pattern intact. The paper can also leave bits caught between the nails and wood that have to be removed with tweezers.

- **Rain's Preferred Method:** Tap pattern dots with a single nail, then remove the pattern before driving in each nail. Start by gripping a single nail in a pair of pliers. This will be the nail that marks each dot. Place the tip of the nail over each dot and gently bop the nail with the hammer; just enough to poke a hole in the wood. When the pattern is removed, the holes in the board will indicate where to drive in nails.

USE PLIERS!

To save your fingers and sanity while nailing, use a pair of trusty needle-nose pliers to hold the nail while hammering. It's easier to see the pattern dots, and the pliers can measure how deep each nail is driven into the board. Hat tip to my dad for providing this idea and also giving me his pliers.

To use pliers to measure your nail depth, first grip a nail in the pliers and sink the nail to the desired length. Then, slide the pliers so that they are gently wedged between the board and the head of the nail. Use a pencil to mark the side of the pliers where the nail head is resting (see above). You now have an easy tool to make sure that your nails are evenly tapped into the board.

If you have a crooked nail set into the board, please use *pliers* to move it. Do *not* attempt to hit the side of the nail with the hammer to straighten it out. This could 1) hurt you or 2) ruin the board. Don't use the board for leverage, or the pliers could scratch the wood.

Transferring Paint Patterns

Several patterns in this book involve painted elements such as eyes, lettering, or leaves. There are two ways to transfer the designs.

- **Carbon Paper:** Layer carbon paper under the pattern on the board. Tape pattern into place. Trace elements with a pencil to transfer the lines onto the board via the carbon paper. Slip the carbon paper out from under the pattern and discard; keep the pattern taped in place and move on to nailing.

- **MacGyver It:** Make a copy of the pattern. Trace elements on the back side of the pattern with a pencil, getting liberal with the amount of graphite on the paper. Tape the pattern in place, and then rub the front of the paper to transfer the graphite to the board.

Stringing the Patterns

Project instructions indicate which direction to wrap the string around each nail. After the first few projects, clockwise is abbreviated as cl and counterclockwise is abbreviated as cc. Stringing sequences may continue in the next paragraph or page of instructions. Do not tie off or cut thread until instructed.

Finishing

After each project is strung, tie-on and tie-off nails will have threads hanging from them. Clip threads to ½ inch in length and then apply rubber cement or white glue to the string; push it toward the design, making your best attempt to cleverly hide it under the design strings on the nail. I prefer rubber cement because it is easier to control, and dried bits can be dusted away with an eraser. This is perhaps the most tedious task in string art, but makes the design look polished.

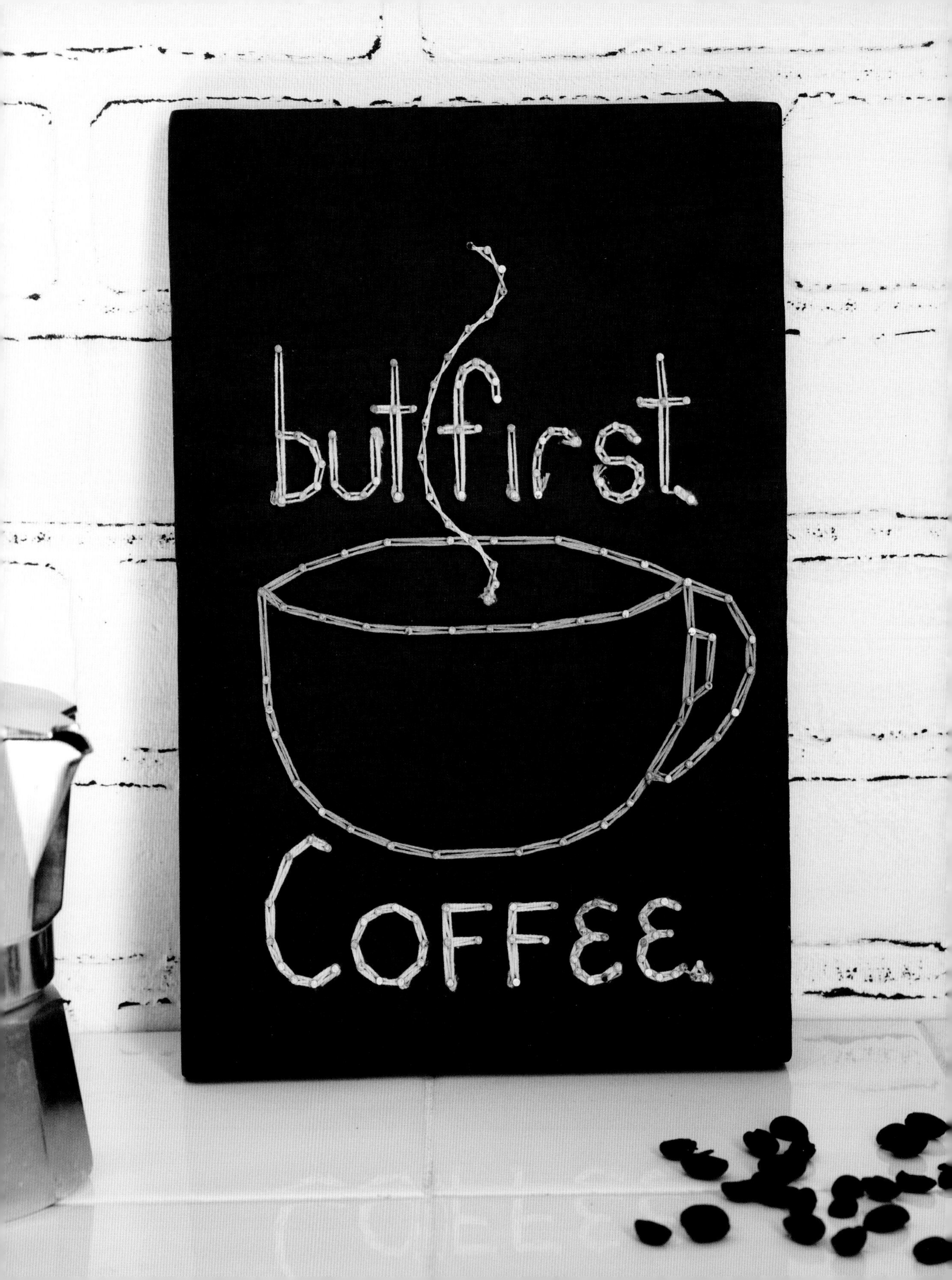
but first
COFFEE

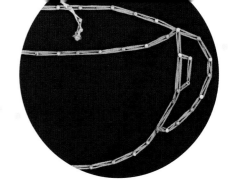

BUT FIRST...COFFEE

Here you are, at what I hope will be your first string art project of many. This initial project is the quickest and easiest to complete in the book and will help you get used to working with wood, nails, and string.

This design honors the beverage that made this book possible. If you are a morning person, then you possess a mystical power that I could never master. For those of us who need a little help, this sign reminds your guests that all questions come after caffeine.

If you're more of a tea drinker, consult the available lettering in the appendix (page 120) and replace the letters with your own message. Might I suggest: "Tea, Earl Grey. Hot."

MATERIALS

- Wooden board of choice, at least 7 x 11 x ¾ in.
- Dark wood stain
- 177 nails, ½-in. length
- Embroidery thread in the following colors:
    - Teal, ½ skein
    - Silver, ½ skein
    - White, ½ skein
- Rubber cement or white glue

TOOLS

- Large-grit sandpaper
- Paintbrush or rag for stain
- Tape
- Hammer
- Needle-nose pliers
- Scissors

THE LESSON

outlines

Simple nail-to-nail outlines should not be overlooked as an element of string art style. The weight of outlines can help define and polish the look of the final work. Outline fundamentals will serve you in all string art projects moving forward.

Wrapping clockwise or counterclockwise around the next nail in the pattern drastically changes the weight of the outline. Experiment with wrapping in either direction as you work through this project.

Types of Wraps

ZIGZAG

Weave the thread around alternating sides of the nails; on the left side of the first, and the right side of the next.

SINGLE

Wrap the thread once completely around the nail before moving on. You can choose clockwise or counterclockwise.

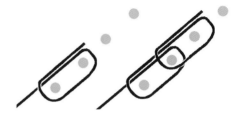

OPEN

Circle the thread around the first and second nails, then back to the first nail to create an outline on both sides. Continue on by using one of the nails you just wrapped and the next open one.

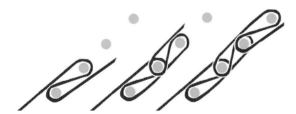

SLASH

Run the thread past a nail, then around the next and back in an S shape that encompasses the skipped nail; this adds a diagonal thread in between an open outline to give it more weight.

BARN DOOR

Create a figure 8 around two nails, then an outline around the outside of them. Continue by using the just-wrapped nail and the adjacent unwrapped nail. This design adds another slash to create an X in the open outline; the most solid line possible between two nails.

BOARD PREP

1. Sand the edges of the board and apply a layer of dark wood stain according to package directions. Let dry at least 8 hours.

2. Stain one more time for an even coat. Let dry overnight.

3. Copy or remove the pattern from the book (page 92).

4. Trim off the outside blank area of the pattern. Tape the pattern to the wood and hammer in nails using desired method (see page 21).

CUP: SLASH OUTLINE

1. Using teal thread, tie a double knot onto nail #5, leaving an inch-long tail of string.

2. Loop clockwise around #6.

3. Go back to wrap counterclockwise around #5.

4. Pass #6 along the top and loop clockwise over #7.

5. Loop counterclockwise over #6.

6. Repeat the slash outline pattern to #8 and then back to #5 around the lip of the cup.

7. Continue slash outline from #5 to #8, this time around the bottom of the cup.

8. Continue slash outline from #8 to #9 around the outside of the handle.

9. Continue slash outline from #9 to #10, up the inside of the handle, ending at #11. Tie off and trim thread.

STEAM: ZIGZAG OUTLINE

1. Using silver thread, tie onto one end of the steam wisp.

2. Using the zigzag outline, wrap to the left side of the next nail, then the right side of the following nail. Repeat this pattern all the way up the steam.

3. Wrap on the opposite sides back down the steam to the bottom. Tie off and trim thread.

"BUT FIRST": OPEN OUTLINE

1. Using white thread, tie on to nail #1.

2. Wrap counterclockwise around #2.

3. Loop back to #1, pass underneath #2, and wrap counterclockwise around #3.

4. Wrap counterclockwise around #2.

5. Wrap once around #3 before moving onto #4. This is because the letter curves, so the string needs to stop at #3 instead of continuing to #4 as usual in an open outline, or it will create an angle of string where we don't want it. Keep an eye on curves when completing an open outline. Make these "pit stops" to prevent unwanted angles.

Continue with the first letter. When you complete it, tie off and trim the thread. Tie on to the beginning of the next letter and continue, tying off and trimming the thread when each letter is done.

"COFFEE": BARN DOOR OUTLINE

1. Using white thread, tie on to nail #12.

2. Wrap clockwise around #13.

3. Wrap counterclockwise around #12.

4. Wrap counterclockwise around #13 and #12.

5. Pass #13 and wrap counterclockwise around #14.

6. Wrap clockwise around #13.

7. Wrap counterclockwise around #14.

8. Wrap counterclockwise around #13.

9. Skip #14 and wrap counterclockwise around #15.

10. Continue this wrapping pattern around each letter, tying off and trimming the thread at the completion of each.

11. Glue down the trimmed ends of the thread.

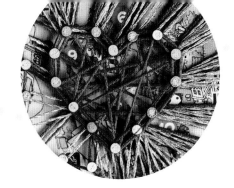

STATE SCRAPBOOK

Chances are, one of the first freeform string art designs you ever ran into was of a state. Perhaps it's the rustic nature of nails, board, and string that inspire a nostalgic nod toward home, or maybe it's just the gift shop appeal that keeps crafters producing these shapes. Whatever the motive, it never hurts to be reminded of where you came from.

I grew up near an amusement park called Kings Island, where I cut my thrill-seeker teeth on record-breaking roller coasters. By applying an old Kings Island park map underneath my Ohio string art, I'm hoping to create a more original design that reminds me not just of Ohio, but of summer days spent struggling to keep down my blue ice cream after a ride on The Beast.

MATERIALS

- Wooden board of choice, at least 8 x 8 x ¾ in.
- About 100 nails (depending on chosen state/icons), ½-in. length
- Embroidery thread in the following colors:
  - Salmon (or color of choice), ½ skein
  - Silver metallic (or color of choice), ½ skein
- Map, printed photos, or other scrapbooking material of choice
- Decoupage glue
- Rubber cement or white glue

TOOLS

- Large-grit sandpaper
- Tape
- Hammer
- Needle-nose pliers
- Scissors

THE LESSON

organized freeform

Not all freeform string art is random. In this design, we deliberately create rays of string radiating away from the heart. The salmon thread is used sparingly so that we can see more of the map underneath. What you do with this design is your choice; I've included heart, star, and house icons, but the placement, fill, and outline of these shapes is up to you.

BOARD PREP

1. I've used a map in my design, but any paper material could work. Consider a collage of tickets, photos, a menu, or whatever else tickles your fancy. This project can act as a mini scrapbook to hang on the wall, so make it personal.

2. Choose thread that complements the colors of your chosen background. Just remember to choose a bright one to be used sparingly (salmon in my project) and one that is subtler (silver in my project).

3. Copy or remove the icon patterns of choice from the book (page 93). Find a map or do an Internet search for the state, country, or other location you'd like to feature. Trace an outline of the map to use as your pattern.

4. Cut out the icon and refer to a state map to correctly place it over the city or landmark that you'd like to commemorate. Tape in place over the state pattern and nail using chosen method (page 21).

STATE RAYS

1. Tie both the colors of thread onto the upper left corner of the icon.

2. String to the upper-left corner of the state, then back to the same nail on the icon.

3. Next, string only the silver thread back out from the icon to the next nail on the edge of the state. Return to the same nail on the icon.

4. String again from icon to state on the next few state nails using only the silver thread.

5. Once back at the icon, string both threads from the first nail on the icon to the second nail.

6. Go out again to the next nail on the edge of the state with both threads, then back to the second icon nail.

7. Repeat this method of stringing to create the rays. Skip nails on the state as needed to create an even design. Use your judgment on how to evenly space the salmon (bright) thread with the silver (subtler) thread.

ICON

1. Tie off and trim silver thread after the rays are finished. Work salmon thread around the icon randomly. I like to string to a nail, then the one next to it, then to a nail on the opposite side. This creates a lot of quick triangles.

2. Return to the upper-left nail where the thread was originally tied on.

3. Open outline (page 26) around the icon and back to that nail.

4. Tie off and trim.

5. Use glue to attach the thread ends to the nails.

AHOY MATEY

When I was living in Ohio, I dedicated our entire bathroom décor to my love of the sea, embellishing with wooden whales, rope nets, and a few shells along the sink. I was a thousand miles from the beach, but when I was in the shower, I could almost hear the waves crashing. Or maybe that was the toilet flushing—it's difficult for moms to ever be truly alone with their beach thoughts.

adding elements

This anchor is constructed so that the strings trap a collection of seashells, but I hope that you use it as inspiration to create your own shapes and fillers. The key is to be sure that you have multiple layers of string on the tall nails to trap your filler on the sides; also zigzag the string across the top of the design enough to trap the filler, but not so much that you obscure it.

MATERIALS

- Wooden board of choice, at least 9 x 8 x ¾ in.
- 135 white nails, 1 ¼-in. length
- Two handfuls of shells that are 1 to 1 ½ in. long
- Embroidery thread in the following colors:
    - White, ½ skein
    - Blue, ½ skein
    - Variegated white and blue, ½ skein
- White paint
- Rubber cement or white glue

TOOLS

- Large-grit sandpaper
- Paintbrush
- Tape
- Hammer
- Needle-nose pliers
- Scissors

BOARD PREP

1. Sand the edges of the board.

2. Brush lightly with white paint.

3. Smudge the paint with your hand, creating a worn look, or wait until it dries and rub with small-grain sandpaper; 150 grit will work.

4. When paint is dry, hammer in nails using chosen method (page 21). The pattern is on page 94.

FIRST LAYER

1. Tie white thread halfway up the nail of the anchor point marked #1.

2. Wrap a single outline around every outer nail on the anchor. Here, you are creating a fence that will keep the shells from slipping through the nails.

3. Tie off and trim the thread when you get back to the starting nail.

TOP LOOP

1. Tie blue thread onto a nail on the interior loop at the top of the anchor.

2. Slash outline (page 26) all around the circle.

3. Tie off and trim the thread.

SHELL FILL

Fill the anchor with the shells, carefully arranging them so that they take up the entire space. Place small shells in cozy spots like the points at the bottom of the anchor. Fit them together like a puzzle so that they will not shift once your creation is hung up on the wall.

NET

1. Tie variegated thread onto one of the points of the anchor.

2. Begin crisscrossing over the shells, wrapping the thread around various nails to build up a net of string. Take care to keep your coverage even, but also zigzag more where you think a shell may try to escape.

3. Tie off and trim the thread when you are satisfied with your net.

OUTLINE

1. Tie blue thread onto one of the points of the anchor.

2. Weave an open outline all around the anchor.

3. Tie off and trim the thread. Use rubber cement or glue to adhere all thread tails to the nails.

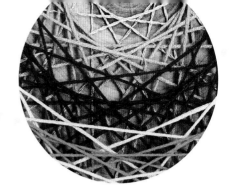

RAINBOW MANDALA

The hypnotizing patterns of mandalas are said to calm the mind and poise the spirit for renewal. This pattern is so easy that you won't only gain a sense of peace from it, you'll feel pretty darned accomplished, too.

While this pattern looks very complicated, it's achieved with little more skill than the ability to count to ten. Here you'll catch on to the idea that geometric string art, while intricate, is really just the repetition of many simple angles.

THE LESSON

circular patterns

By simply skipping nails while working in the round, it is possible to create varying circle sizes that can be stacked on top of each other. In pictorial string art, these circle shapes are used for everything from eyeballs to blooming flowers. As you string this project, the sequence of skipping will quickly become evident, and I'm confident you'll soon be able to create your own circular designs.

MATERIALS

- Birch round with bark, about 8-in. diameter and ¾-in. thick
- Embroidery thread in the following colors:
  - Silver, ½ skein
  - Light purple, ½ skein
  - Dark purple, ½ skein
  - Dark blue, ½ skein
  - Light blue, ½ skein
  - Green, ½ skein
  - Yellow, ½ skein
  - Yellow-orange, ½ skein
  - Orange, ½ skein
  - Red, ½ skein
- 26 nails, 1-in. length
- Rubber cement or white glue

TOOLS

- Large-grit sandpaper
- Tape
- Hammer
- Needle-nose pliers
- Scissors

BOARD PREP

1. This design is so complex that the board itself is pretty simple. I used a thick birch round from my local craft store. Sand the surface smooth if needed.

2. Using the pattern from page 95 and nailing method of choice (page 21), add the circle of 26 nails to the round.

NOTES TO KEEP IN MIND

1. Single wrap clockwise around each nail throughout this pattern.

2. You will notice that the even-numbered layers have more points to tie on. This is a result of the even numbers dividing well into the 26 nails, thus producing more spans of string. Plot the colors of your mandala accordingly if choosing your own; bolder colors will do best on the odd-numbered layers.

LAYER 1: SKIP 11

Tie silver thread onto #1. Skip 11 nails clockwise to wrap around #13. Continue the pattern of skipping 11 nails until the thread ends up back at #1. The entire sequence is #1-13-25-11-23-9-21-7-19-5-17-3-15-1.

LAYER 2: SKIP 10

Tie light purple thread onto #2. Skip 10 nails clockwise to wrap around #13. The entire sequence is #2-13-24-9-20-5-16-1-12-23-8-19-4-15-26-11-22-7-18-3-14-25-10-21-6-17-2.

LAYER 3: SKIP 9

Tie dark purple thread onto #3. Skip 9 nails clockwise to wrap around #13. The entire sequence is #3-13-23-7-17-1-11-21-5-15-25-9-19-3.

LAYER 4: SKIP 8

Tie dark blue thread onto #4. Skip 8 nails clockwise to wrap around #13. The entire sequence is #4-13-22-5-14-23-6-15-24-7-16-25-8-17-26-9-18-1-10-19-2-11-20-3-12-21-4.

LAYER 5: SKIP 7

Tie light blue thread onto #5. Skip 7 nails clockwise to wrap around #13. The entire sequence is #5-13-21-3-11-19-1-9-17-25-7-15-23-5.

LAYER 6: SKIP 6

Tie green thread onto #6. Skip 6 nails clockwise to wrap around #13. The entire sequence is #6-13-20-1-8-15-22-3-10-17-24-5-12-19-26-7-14-21-2-9-16-23-4-11-18-25-6.

LAYER 7: SKIP 5

Tie yellow thread onto #7. Skip 5 nails clockwise to wrap around #13. The entire sequence is #7-13-19-25-5-11-17-23-3-9-15-21-1-7.

LAYER 8: SKIP 4

Tie yellow-orange thread to #8. Skip 4 nails to wrap around #13. The entire sequence is #8-13-18-23-2-7-12-17-22-1-6-11-16-21-26-5-10-15-20-25-4-9-14-19-24-3-8.

LAYER 9: SKIP 3

Tie orange thread to #9. Skip 3 nails to wrap around #13. The entire sequence is #9-13-17-21-25-3-7-11-15-19-23-1-5-9.

LAYER 10: SKIP 2

Tie red thread onto #10. Skip 2 nails to #13. The entire sequence is #10-13-16-19-22-25-2-5-8-11-14-17-20-23-26-3-6-9-12-15-18-21-24-1-4-7-10.

FINISHING

The threads can be cut off or left to hang long in a cascading rainbow. This is especially impressive on mandalas that have many nails. If you do cut off the threads, be sure to glue down the ends.

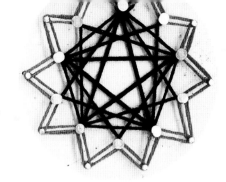

SUGAR SKULL

In Mexico, it is believed that the dearly departed return to the mortal realm on Día de Muertos to thumb their noses at death and enjoy sweet offerings from us mere mortals.

Before you chuck candy and run, the idea is less *Scooby Doo* and more "supporting spirits in navigating the afterlife." Sugar skulls provide mystical cuteness for the otherwise morbid celebration, adding a burst of color to quell the dreariness of Halloween. In this spirit, get ready to make your own Mr. Potato Skull!

combining simple shapes

This sugar skull is an example of a string art design that brings together simple shapes to create a pictorial. I've provided various shapes for you to create your own creepy compadre on pages 96 and 97. These are very easy to string, so it's easy to get creative by making your own shapes, too.

MATERIALS

- Circular board, at least 6 ½-in. diameter and ¾-in. thick
- White paint
- About 100 wire brads, ¾-in. length (depending on patterns selected)
- About 60 nails, ½-in. length (depending on patterns selected)
- Embroidery thread in the following colors:
    - Black, ½ skein
    - Pink, ½ skein
    - Yellow, ½ skein
    - Orange, ½ skein
- Rubber cement or white glue

TOOLS

- Large-grit sandpaper
- Foam brush
- Tape
- Hammer
- Needle-nose pliers
- Scissors

BOARD PREP

1. Get the skull pattern from page 96. The painted skull shape is a background that pulls the entire work together. The use of paint to balance a string art design can cut down on strung elements and offer integral pops of color. The paper around our cut patterns is typically discarded, but this time, trim carefully and save the extra paper to create a stencil. Set skull pattern aside.

2. Center and tape the skull stencil to the board.

3. Dab on white paint with a foam brush. Fill in the skull shape completely, and then remove the stencil. Let paint dry completely.

4. Select the features you like best from pages 96 and 97. I used the flower cap, green leaf embellishments, teardrop forehead embellishment, X spots, mandala eyes, heart nose, and teeth. Tape the skull pattern shapes to the board, using a ruler to evenly place symmetrical features.

5. Tap in brads on the small dots, and nails on the large dots.

INNER MANDALA EYES

1. Tie black thread to #1. The first pattern around the eye, counterclockwise, will skip 3 nails. The entire sequence is #1-7-3-9-5-1.

2. Continue moving around the eye counterclockwise, this time skipping 2 nails. The entire sequence is #8-5-2-9-6-3-10-7-4-1.

3. For the last layer, continue counterclockwise, skipping 1 nail. The entire sequence is #9-7-5-3-1.

4. Tie off and cut the thread. Scoot the black thread down on the nails to leave the upper half of the nail free.

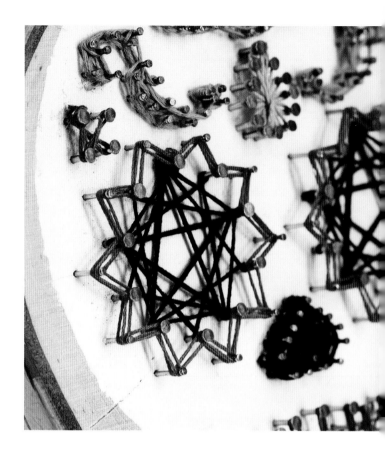

OUTER MANDALA EYES

1. Tie pink thread onto nail #3.

2. Use an open outline around the eyes, following the shape on the pattern.

3. Tie off at #3.

EYELASH EYES

1. Tie black thread to #1. Wrap each nail counterclockwise in single wrap outline from #1 to #2.

2. Wrap back to #1, this time along top side of nails.

3. Open outline from #3-4-3.

4. Single outline back to #1. Tie off.

DIAMOND EYES

1. With purple thread, tie on to #1.
2. Wrapping counterclockwise, open outline from #1-2-1-2-3-2-3-4-3-4-1-4.
3. Wrap counterclockwise around #5 to start the second diamond.
4. Repeat the open outline wrapping pattern to complete the second diamond.
5. Tie off at #5.

TRIANGLE EYES

1. With red thread, tie on to #1.
2. String an open outline with this sequence: #1-3-1-2-1.
3. Single wrap outline down the right leg of the triangle to #8.
4. String an open outline with this sequence: #8-7-8-9-8.
5. Single wrap outline along the bottom leg of the triangle to #4.
6. String an open outline with this sequence: #4-6-4-5-4.
7. Single wrap outline up the left leg of the triangle to 1. Tie off.

FLOWER CAP BUD

1. The inner part of the flower is like a ray of light. Make sure the thread is an open wrap (see page 26 for description of open versus closed outline wraps). Tie yellow thread onto #1.
2. Wrap around #2, then back to #1. Proceed to #3-1-4-1.
3. Repeat pattern to #10.
4. Open outline wrap across the top from #10 to #2. Tie off.

FLOWER CAP PETALS

1. Tie orange thread to #11 and freeform fill to the right. Fill in the petals as desired, zigzagging the thread to fill each petal before moving on to the next petal to the right.
2. Open outline on outside of petals from #10 back to #11. Tie off.

HEART AND LEAVES CAP

Fill heart and leaves freeform style with red and green thread.

DIAMOND CAP

Fill diamond cap freeform style. This piece is a great space to experiment with various outlines.

HEART NOSE

1. With black thread, tie on to #1.
2. Freeform fill diagonally, then vertically, then horizontally across brads.
3. End fill at #1.
4. Single wrap outline all around nose and end again at #1. Tie off.

TRIANGLE NOSE

1. With black thread, tie on to #1.
2. String an open outline style of wrap counterclockwise to #2 and back to #1.
3. Continue stringing counterclockwise: #3-4-3-5-6-5.
4. Single outline around each: #7-2-4-6.
5. Wrap clockwise around #4.
6. Open outline from #4 back to #1. Tie off.

TEETH

1. Tie purple thread on to #1.

2. Wrap around #2.

3. Open outline over #3 and #4.

4. Return to #2.

5. Move to the next brad to the right and repeat the pattern.

6. Repeat pattern across teeth, working an open outline vertically over the nails and a single wrap between the teeth. Tie off at #5.

LIPS

1. With red, tie on to #1.

2. Fill lips freeform style, returning to #1.

3. Open outline from #1 all around lips.

4. Return to #1 and tie off.

TEARDROP FOREHEAD EMBELLISHMENT

1. Tie blue thread on to #1.

2. Wrap around #2-3-4-5-6.

3. Continue pattern of wrapping the next nail in sequence until the thread is returned to nail #1.

4. Tie off at #1.

GREEN LEAVES EMBELLISHMENT

1. This greenery is freeform with practice in backstitching the edges as the work is completed. As the brads are filled with thread, take care to backstitch before moving to the next area. Tie green thread onto the end of the leaf at #1.

2. Work freehand through the leaf shape.

3. Use a single outline around the leaf as it is filled.

X SPOTS

1. The X points are a short exercise in learning to start and end a design at the same spot. See if you can navigate the X as the pattern shows to begin and end on the same nail. Tie onto one X point and work to the diagonal point.

2. Wrap to the point across.

3. Wrap to the other diagonal point.

4. End at the same point and tie off.

EVENING STAR

"When you wish upon a star, makes no difference who you are.
Anything your heart desires, will come to you."
—Walt Disney's *Pinocchio*

Shooting your intentions into the atmosphere certainly can't hurt, but it's the work behind the wish that turns dreams into reality. My father, who is a very different man than Walt, sang his own version: "When you spit upon a star . . . you are spitting pretty far."

My sisters and I certainly gave that activity our best effort, but I'd like to think that dear ol' dad was trying to pass on a lesson about hard work. I hope this wishing star and crescent moon can serve as a reminder to put some muscle behind those dreams.

Note: This pattern uses a few different nail and brad sizes to keep the star and moon in proportion to each other.

MATERIALS

- Circular board, 16-in. diameter and ¾-in. thick
- 59 nails, ½-in. length
- 88 wire brads, ¾-in. length
- 1 nail, 1-in. length
- Embroidery thread in the following colors:
  - Yellow, 2 skeins
  - Metallic silver, ½ skein
  - Turquoise, ½ skein
- Decoupage materials, such as painted paper, photos, or colored paper
- Decoupage glue
- White glue or rubber cement

TOOLS

- Large-grit sandpaper
- Tape
- Hammer
- Needle-nose pliers
- Scissors

THE LESSON

forming cardioids

The outline of the crescent moon in this project is mathematically known as a "cardioid." This heart shape occurs when a curve is traced by a point on the circumference of an identical circle. Clear as mud, right?

Okay, imagine you have two plates of equal size placed side-by-side on a white tablecloth. There is a little jelly on the bottom of the plates where the edges touch. You begin to rotate one plate around the other, resulting in a line of jelly traced on the tablecloth. When your plate has returned to its original position, you've drawn a cardioid. Then, the waitress asks you to leave.

BOARD PREP

1. I've decoupaged pieces of colored paper to the front of my board to create an interstellar stained glass. This is optional, as you can paint the board or glue fabric to it, instead. Maintain a galactic mood with a dark blue or black background on the wood that will contrast well with metallic and lightly shaded threads.

2. Get pattern from pages 98 to 101 and assemble on the crosshairs. Center the pattern on the board and tape at the edges.

3. At the #1 dot on the star, drive the 1-inch nail into the board. Tap ¾-inch wire brads into place on the rest of the evening star. Drive the ½-inch nails around the 59 dots in the circle.

CRESCENT MOON

1. Check your string art against the pattern to make sure your lines are correct. Pay special attention to the cluster of strings in the middle. Strings out-of-place in the middle of your string art can quickly indicate a misstep in the pattern.

2. Tie yellow thread onto #45. Wrap cc to #46-47-17-16-15-14-13-41-40-39-12-11-37-36-35-10-9-33-32-31-8-7-29-28-27-6-5-25-24-3-2-1-23-22-58-57-56-21-20-54-53-52-19-18-51-50-49-17-16-15-14-43-44-45.

3. Continue: cc #1-2-46-47-3-4-48-49-5-6-50-51-7-8-52-53-9-10-54-55-11-12-56-57-13-14-58-59-15-16-17-1-2-19-20-21-3-4-23-24-25-5-6-7-26-27-9-10-11-28-29-13-14-15-30-31-17-18-19-32-33-21-22-23-34-35-24-25-36-37-26-27-38-39-28-29-40-41-30-31-42-43-32-33-44-45. Tie off.

EVENING STAR: LAYER 1

1. Tie metallic silver thread onto #1. Wrap cc to #8-9-10, cl #1-25-24-23, cc #1-38-39-40, cl #1-55-54-53.

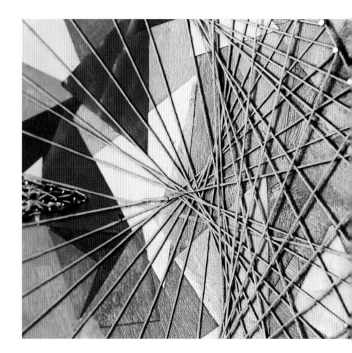

2. Continue: cc #1-56-57, cl #1-37-36, cc #1-41-42, cl #1-22-21, cc #1-26-27, cl #1-7-6, cc #1-12-11, cl #1-52-51.

3. Continue: cc #1-4-5, cl #1-14-13, cc #1-50-49, cl #1-59-58, cc #1-34-35, cl #1-44-43, cc #1-19-20, cl #1-29-28.

4. Continue: cc #1-2-3, cl #1-16-15, cc #1-47-48, cl #1-61-60, cc #1-32-33, cl #1-46-45, cc #1-17-18, cl #1-31-30-1. Tie off.

EVENING STAR: LAYER 2

1. The next sequence will create emphasis on each of the outer points. Tie turquoise thread onto #85.

2. Wrap cc to #55-56-48-49-57-58-50-51-59-60-52-53-87.

3. Continue: #40-41-33-34-42-43-35-36-44-45-37-38-88.

4. Continue: #25-26-18-19-27-28-20-21-30-29-23-22-86.

5. Continue: #10-11-3-4-12-13-5-6-14-15-8-7-85. Tie off.

SWEDISH BLOOMS

"Oh, tiptoe from the garden,
by the garden of the willow tree
and tiptoe through the tulips with me."
—Tiny Tim

Most standard string art shapes can be turned into blooms. The varying petals, leaves, and stems offer plenty of inspiration for string art design. When working with shapes or methods that are new to you, a flower pictorial can be a good place to start. Before you know it, you can assemble many shapes into an entire garden of geometric design.

symmography sampler

This project is a style of sampler that displays various patterns of stringing in one overall design. The flowers feature repeating patterns that are quick to pick up on the first petal, and can be reused in your own designs.

MATERIALS

- Wooden board of choice, at least 12 x 12 x ¾ in.
- White paint
- Carbon paper or pencil
- Light green paint
- 274 nails, ½-in. length
- Embroidery thread in the following colors:
  - Red, ¼ skein
  - Pink, ¼ skein
  - Yellow, ½ skein
  - Yellow-orange, ¼ skein
  - Lavender, 1 skein
  - Purple, ¼ skein
  - Turquoise, ¼ skein
  - Denim blue, ¼ skein
  - Light green, ⅛ skein
- Rubber cement or white glue

TOOLS

- Large-grit sandpaper
- Paintbrush
- Tape
- Hammer
- Needle-nose pliers
- Scissors

BOARD PREP

1. Paint the board white. Let dry and the edges to distress, especially at the corners.

2. Get the pattern from pages 102 to 103. Transfer the leaves using the instructions on page 23. Paint the leaves light green.

POPPY

1. Tie red thread onto #1. Wrap cc to #2-3-4-5-6-7-8-9-10. Repeat pattern around the flower. #10 becomes #1 for the next petal.

2. Outline all around the octagon, as shown in the pattern. Tie off at the original #1.

3. Tie pink thread onto #1. Wrap cc to #6-1-10-5-10. Repeat this pattern all the way around the poppy, returning to #1. Tie off.

DAISY

1. Tie yellow thread onto #1. Wrap cc to #6-2-7-3-8-4-9-5-10-6-11-7-12-8-13-9-14-1.

2. #15 now becomes #1 in the pattern. Repeat the previous wrapping sequence in each petal, back around to the original #1. Tie off.

3. Tie yellow-orange thread onto #1. Open outline all the way around the daisy, returning to #1. Tie off.

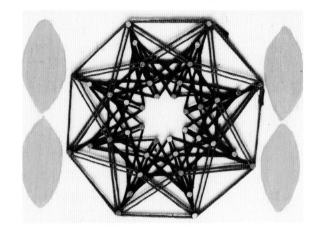

LILY

1. Tie lavender thread onto #1. Wrap cl from #1-2-3-4-5-6-7-8-9-10-11-12-13-14-15-16-17-18-19.

2. #19 turns into #1 on the next petal. Repeat pattern all the way around. Tie off on last petal's #19.

3. Tie purple thread onto #1 and open outline all the way around. Tie off back at #1.

ROSE

1. First petal: Tie turquoise thread onto #1. Wrap cc to #1-2-1-2-11-12, cl #3-13-4-14-5-15-6-16-7-17-8-18-9-19-10.

2. Second petal: cl #21-9-22-8-23-7-24-6-25-5-26-4-27-3-28-2-29-30-29.

3. Third petal: cc #12-28-13-27-14-26-15-25-16-24-17-23-18-22-19-21-20. Tie off.

4. Repeat this method of stringing to complete the last three petals, using a denim blue thread.

DANDELION

1. Tie light green thread on to #1. Wrap from #1-2-1-3-1-4-1-5.

2. Repeat pattern, moving around the dandelion. Return to #1 and tie off.

3. Glue down all thread ends with glue or rubber cement.

VANISHING CHESHIRE CAT

Does this sign describe the crew at your house? I've found that if I just remind myself that my family is crazy, then I can't really expect my son to stop sleeping in an old cardboard box by his bed. He's 14. A 20-foot dragon guards our house, my husband is known for streaking, and one of our treasured family songs is about amoebas on the subway. Normal to us, but others are sometimes bemused. Then again, I keep hair clippings from all my family members and eat tartar sauce by the spoonful . . . As the Cheshire Cat disappears, he leaves you with a valuable reality check; you're just as nuts as the rest of 'em. Would you really have it any other way?

THE LESSON
use paint instead

We've caught the infamous Cheshire Cat disintegrating into madness, most likely after giving bad directions to lost children. He's never around for long, so a solid shape isn't right for him. I used painted elements to fill in the shape, and mixed freeform with geometric string art because Cheshire is a mixed-up kind of character.

MATERIALS

- Wooden board of choice, at least 7 ¼ x 10 ¼ x ¾ in.
- Black paint
- Carbon paper or pencil
- White paint
- Glow-in-the-dark paint
- 157 nails, ½-in. length
- 48 nails, ¾-in. length
- Embroidery thread in the following colors:
  - Yellow, ¼ skein
  - White, ¼ skein
  - Purple, ½ skein
  - Pink, 1 skein
- Rubber cement or white glue

TOOLS

- Large-grit sandpaper
- Paintbrush
- Tape
- Hammer
- Needle-nose pliers
- Scissors

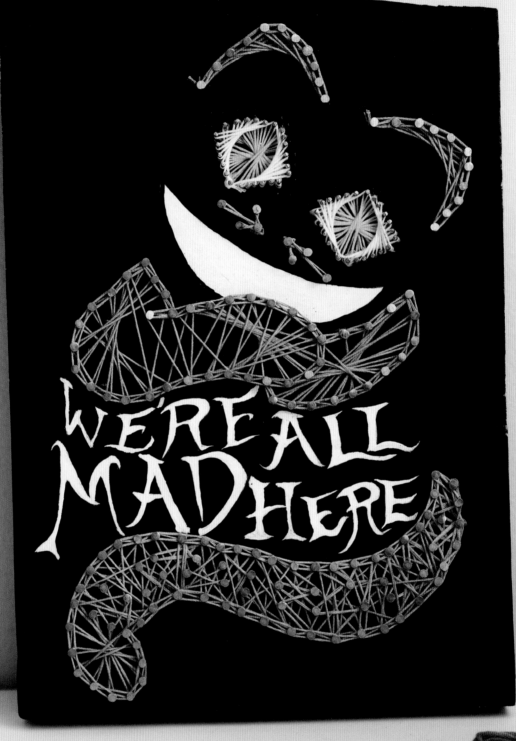

BOARD PREP

1. Paint the board black. Get the pattern from page 114. Transfer the smile and lettering using the instructions on page 23.

2. Using white acrylic paint, fill in the Cheshire Cat's smile with solid paint strokes. Add another coat if needed to fully block out the black paint underneath. Paint the new family motto, "We're All Mad Here," just underneath the arms, as indicated on the pattern.

3. When dry, brush a coat of glow-in-the-dark paint onto the smile.

4. After tacking the pattern holes, remove the paper pattern.

YELLOW INNER EYE

1. Tie yellow onto #1. Wrap cc to #13-2-14-3-15-4-16-5-17-6-18-7-19-8-20-9-21-10-22-11-23-12-24-1. Tie off.

2. Repeat on second eye.

WHITE OUTER EYE

1. Tie white onto #1. Wrap cc to #7-2-8-3-9-4-10-5-11-6-12-19-13-20-14-21-15-22-16-23-17-24-18-1. Tie off.

2. Repeat on second eye.

WHISKERS

1. Tie purple thread onto #95. Wrap cc to #96-95-97-95-98-95. Tie off.

2. Repeat pattern for second set of whiskers.

EARS

1. Tie pink thread onto #25. Wrap cc to #30-26-31-27-32-28-33-29-34-30-35. Open outline back to #25. Tie off.

2. Repeat with second ear.

ARMS

1. Tie pink thread onto #36. Wrap cl to #44-67-43-66-42-64-41-48-40-47-39-46-38-45-37-36-67-66-64-56-63-55-62-54-61-53-60-52-59-51-58-50-57-49.

2. Freeform fill the middle of the arm as much as desired, ending on #49.

3. Cc #49-81, cl to #72-80-71-79-70-77-69-76-68-75-53, cc #74, cl #54-73, cc #55-74-73, cl #56.

4. Barn door outline (page 26) from #56 to #55. Repeat around the left arm back to #56.

5. Barn door outline from #56 around the right arm, ending on #52. Tie off.

TAIL

1. Tie pink thread onto #99. Freeform fill the pink areas as shown on the pattern, ending on #100.

2. Barn door outline back up the bottom of the tail to #99. Tie off.

3. Tie purple thread onto #99. Freeform fill purple areas as shown on the pattern, ending at #100.

4. Wrap cc to #106- 112- 105-111-104-110-103-109-102-108-101-107-100.

5. Barn door outline from #100 around the tail to #110.

6. Continue barn door outline across the top of the tail to #99. Tie off.

7. Glue down all thread ends with glue or rubber cement.

8. Wrap cl to #106, cc #112-105, cl #111, cc #104, cl #110, cc #103, cl #109, cc #102, cl #108, cc #101, cl #107, cc #100.

9. Barn door outline from #100 around the tail to #110.

10. Continue barn door outline across the top of the tail to #99. Tie off.

11. Glue down all thread ends with glue or rubber cement.

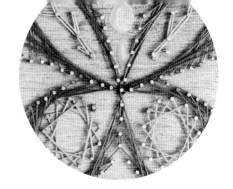

LUCKY BUTTERFLY

It's said that if a butterfly enters your house and flaps around a bit, good luck is sure to follow. I'll take it. If all we have to do is let a fancy bug in the house, then let's open all the windows and play the lottery.

This butterfly board isn't big on fluttering around the room, but she can at least offer an instant display of your stringing prowess to those who come by the house. Front door placement is a bit of a compliment trap, but, hey, hearing your friends compliment your work sure feels close to being lucky. "That ol' thing? Daaahhhhling, I made it." [bats eyelashes]

THE LESSON
open wing design

The teardrop shape of the butterfly's top wings is a popular device for string art patterns. These can be used as petals (see a smaller version in my Swedish Blooms project on page 46), wings, raindrops, and more. It's a useful type of stringing that is easy to duplicate in your own designs, and stringing it twice here will give you the hang of the sequence.

MATERIALS

- Wooden board of choice, at least 14 x 9 x ¾ in.
- Light oak stain
- Carbon paper or pencil
- Yellow paint
- Brown paint
- Green paint
- Blue paint
- 255 nails, ½-in. length
- Embroidery thread in the following colors:
  - Pink, 1 skein
  - Salmon, ½ skein
  - Orange-yellow, ¼ skein
  - Canary yellow, ¼ skein
  - Pale yellow, 1 skein
- Rubber cement or white glue

TOOLS

- Large-grit sandpaper
- Paintbrush
- Tape
- Hammer
- Needle-nose pliers
- Scissors

BOARD PREP

1. This sign is great for placing just in or out of the door, so I recommend using a light stain to protect the finish of the wood. When done, be sure to hang where sun and rain won't wreak havoc on your creation.

2. Get the pattern from pages 104 to 105. Transfer the painted parts of the pattern using the instructions on page 23.

3. Paint the painted areas according to the color shown on the pattern. Let dry.

UPPER LEFT WING

Tie pink thread onto #1. Wrap cc to #17-18-2-3-19-20-4-5-21-22-6-7-23-24-8-9-25-26-10-11-27-28-12-13-29-30-14-15-31-32-16-17-33-34-18-19-35-36-20-21-37-38-22-23-39-40-24-25-41-42-26-27-87-86-28-29-1.

UPPER RIGHT WING

Wrap cl to #58-59-43-44-60-61-45-46-62-63-47-48-64-65-49-50-66-67-51-52-68-69-53-54-70-71-55-56-72-73-57-58-74-75-59-60-76-77-61-62-78-79-63-64-80-81-65-66-82-83-67-68-84-85-69-70-1. Tie off.

BOTTOM LEFT WING

Tie salmon thread onto #1. Wrap cc to #90-91-86-87-92-93-42-88-95-96-89-90-97-98-91-92-99-100-93-94-101-102-95-96-103-104-97-98-105-106-99-100-107-108-101-102-109-110-103-104-111-112-105-106-1.

BOTTOM RIGHT WING

Wrap cl to #115-116-85-84-117-118-83-113-120-121-114-115-122-123-116-117-124-125-118-119-126-127-120-121-128-129-122-123-130-131-124-125-132-133-126-127-109-110-128-129-111-112-130-131-1. Tie off.

WING DOT

1. Tie orange-yellow thread onto any nail in circle. Skip three nails, wrap around fourth nail. Repeat pattern of skipping three nails until returning to the nail that the thread was tied on. Tie off.

2. Repeat this pattern on other wing dot.

WING VEIN

1. Tie canary yellow thread onto #200. Wrap cc to #201-200-202-203-202-204-205-204-206-204-202-200. Tie off.

2. Repeat pattern style on other wing vein.

LETTER E

1. Tie pale yellow thread onto #134. Wrap cc to #137-138-135-136-139-140-137-138-141-144-145-148-149-146-147-144-145-142-143-146, cl to #149.

2. Open outline from #149 to #134. Tie off.

3. Repeat for pattern style for other letter E.

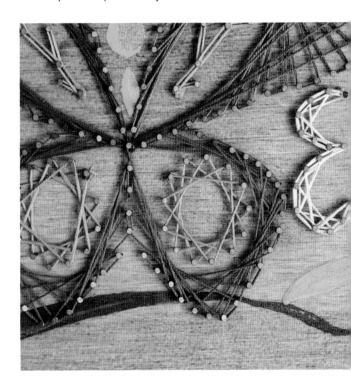

LETTER L

1. Tie pale yellow thread onto #150. Wrap cc to #153-152-155-154-151, cl to #150.

2. Open outline from #150 to #156. Tie off.

LETTER C

1. Tie pale yellow thread onto #157. Wrap cc to #160-159-162-161-158, cl #157.

2. Open outline to #164, cc to #167-166-169-168-165, cl #164.

3. Open outline to #169. Tie off.

LETTER O

1. Tie pale yellow thread onto #170. Wrap cl to #174-175-171-172-176-173-170.

2. Open outline from #170 to #177. Wrap cl to #182-183-178-179-183-184-180-181-177.

3. Open outline from #177 to #170. Tie off.

LETTER M

1. Tie pale yellow thread onto #185. Wrap cl to #186-189-190-186-187-191-192-188-189-192-193-192-195-196-192-191-197-198-194-195-198-199-198, cc #197.

2. Open outline to #187, cc #186-185. Tie off.

3. Glue down all thread ends with glue or rubber cement.

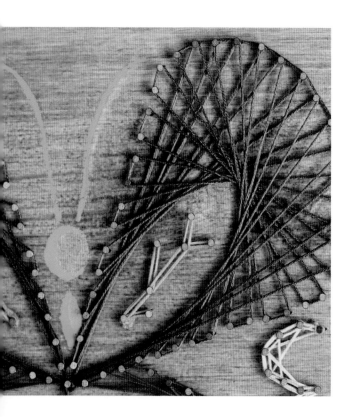

WHICH WAY TO THE BEACH?

Keep a keen eye out along the Gulf Coast, and you may just be lucky enough to spot a quirky coastal primate scuttling between the shade of umbrellas. The lush environment of sea, sand, and walk-up bars is ideal for supplying the North American Redhead's need for curly fries and live music, but a deadly predator looms overhead, ready to sear her blindingly pasty hide to a crisp lobster hue in mere minutes. A ridiculous armor of floppy hats, shawls, and bug-eye sunglasses act as her defense, allowing time to swim and collect shells between ritual slathering of sunblock.

Some of us just weren't made for the beach, but I love it, anyway.

THE LESSON

logarithmic spirals

To create a string art spiral, really all you need to do is skip nails on one side of the circle while stringing to every single nail on the other side. Play with this sequence to create tight or loose spirals. Try skipping three nails on one side, while wrapping every nail on the other. Skip four on one side; skip one on the other. Try changing up the pattern mid-spiral by skipping even more nails. While spirals look complicated, they really are easy to master and allow for a lot of creativity.

MATERIALS

- Wooden board of choice, at least 16 x 10 x ¾ in.
- Decoupage glue
- Rough woven cloth, at least 18 x 12 in.
- 188 nails, ½-in. length
- Embroidery thread in the following colors:
  - Aqua, 1 skein
  - Medium blue, 1 skein
  - Dark blue, ½ skein
  - Yellow, ½ skein
  - White, ¼ skein
- Rubber cement or white glue

TOOLS

- Large-grit sandpaper
- Tape
- Hammer
- Needle-nose pliers
- Scissors

BOARD PREP

1. I covered my board with a piece of burlap-style cloth to give it a coastal look. Cut the burlap 2 inches larger than the board. Sand the edges of the board and brush the face of the board with decoupage glue. Center the board over the cloth and press the sticky face of the board onto the cloth.

2. Brush glue on the sides of the board and wrap the cloth around, clipping at the corners where needed. Paint glue around the back edges and press the cloth down.

3. Let glue dry, then tack the cloth into place by hammering in ½-inch nails at the corners and every few inches.

4. Get pattern from pages 106 to 107 and apply.

AQUA WAVE

Tie aqua thread on to #1. Wrap cc to #55-56-2-3-57-58-4-5-59-60-6-7-62-63-8-9-64-66-10-11-67-68-12-13-70-71-14-15-72-74-16-17-75-76-18-19-78-79-20-21-80-82-22-23-83-84-24-25-86-87-26-27-88-90-28-29-91-94-30-31-95-96-32-33-2-3-34-36. Tie off.

MEDIUM BLUE WAVE

1. The second part of the wave is a darker shade of blue and slips into the water washing ashore. Tie medium blue thread onto #36.

2. Wrap cc to 4-6-37-38-7-8-39-40-9-10-41-42-11-13-43-44-14-16-45-46-17-19-47-48-20-22-49-50-23-25-51-52-26-28-53-55-29-30-56-57-31-32-58-59-33-34-60-62-36-37-63-64-38-39-66-67-40-41-68-70-42-43-71-72-44-45-74-75-46-47-76-78-48-49-79-80-50-51-82-83-52-54-84.

3. Continue out of the circle to create the part of the wave that laps at the shore: #97-98-85-86-99-100-87-88-101-89-102-90-103-91-93-104-93-94-105-94. Tie off.

DARK BLUE WAVE

1. The last layer of the wave is an even darker shade of blue that helps to outline and add dimension to the water. Tie dark blue thread onto #97. Wrap cl to #90-79-78-88-87-76-75-84-83-71-67-81-80-65-62-77-75-59-56-74-73-53-49-71-70-46-42-66-64-39-35-61-58-32-29-55.

2. Wrap cc to #56, then wrap on the outside of the circle from #56-61-69-76-83-90-97. Tie off.

LETTERS

1. For each letter, tie yellow thread onto numbered nail.

2. Slash outline all around as shown in the pattern. Tie off.

ARROW

1. Tie white thread onto #108. Wrap cl to #107-108-106-108-109-110-121.

2. Open outline from #121 to 115 as shown on pattern.

3. Wrap cc to 121.

4. Open outline from #121 to 127 as shown.

5. Wrap cl to #121-110-114-110-111-110-109-113-109-112-109-108.
Tie off.

6. Glue down all thread ends with glue or rubber cement.

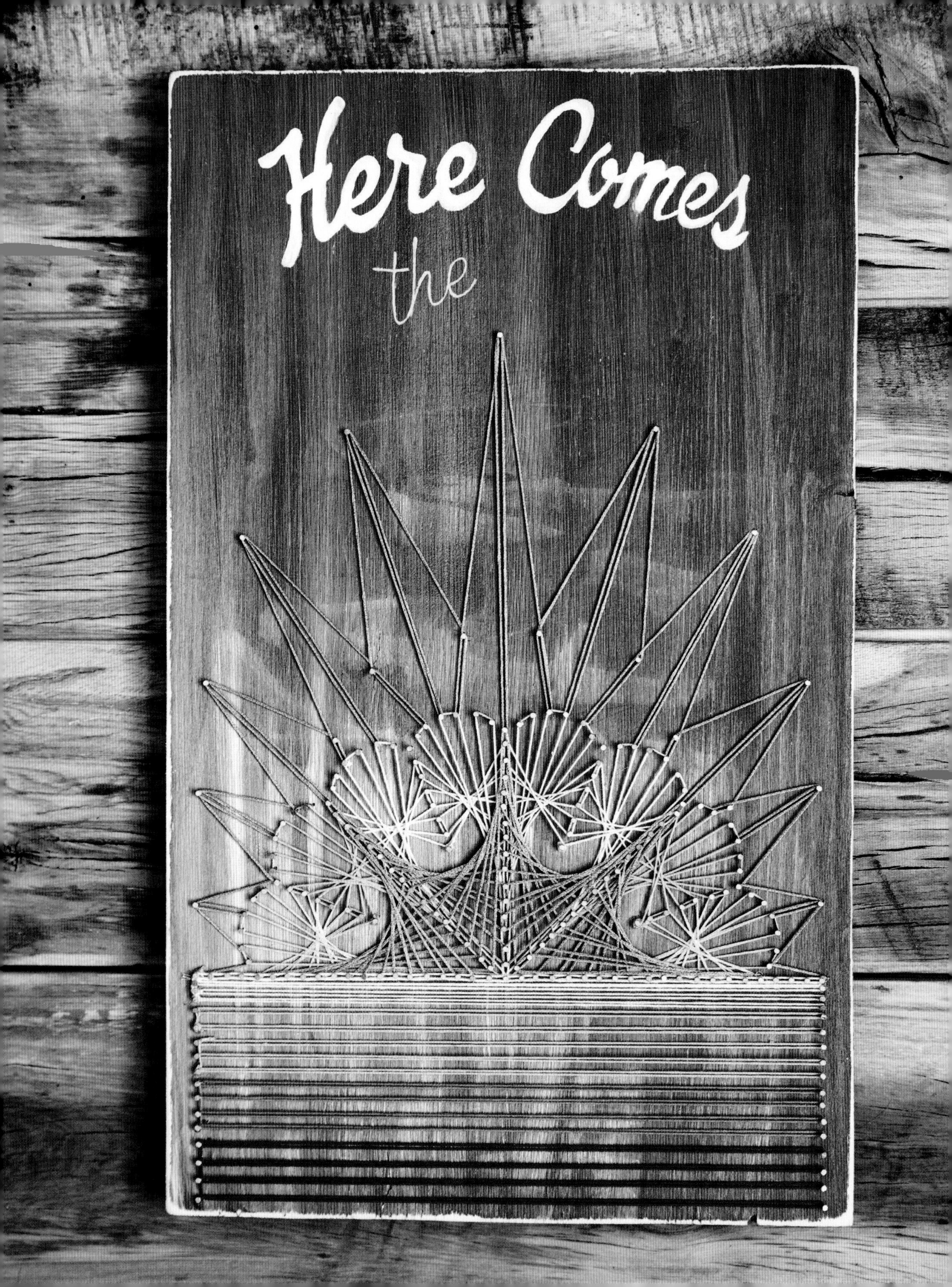
Here Comes
the

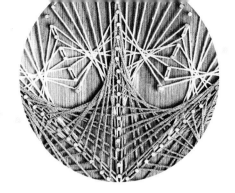

HERE COMES THE SUN

Little darling, it's been a long cold lonely winter
Little darling, it feels like years since it's been here...
—George Harrison

The sun will come out tomorrow; you are my sunshine; and there just ain't no sunshine when she's gone. A giant ball of fiery space gas can really ignite inspiration in the human spirit.

Those lyrics, in turn, have a way of rooting themselves into our psyche and becoming powerful mantras in our lives. If you have the opportunity to incorporate snippets of meaningful sonnets in your string art work, do it; hung on the wall, lyrics can give you that little reminder just when you need it most.

THE LESSON

closed wing design

Opposite of the open wing design found in the Lucky Butterfly project (page 53), this way of wrapping the thread closes the center of the teardrop shapes found in our sun "slices." These shapes are used for wings, scales, and more in pictorial designs. In your own designs, try layering an open wing over a closed wing to create a complex look.

MATERIALS

- Wooden board of choice, at least 11 x 17 ¾ x ¾ in.
- Purple paint
- Red paint
- Orange paint
- Yellow paint
- Carbon paper or pencil
- 120 nails, ½-in. length
- Embroidery thread in the following colors:
    - Metallic gold, 1 skein
    - Canary yellow, ½ skein
    - Light orange, ½ skein
    - Pale yellow, ½ skein
    - Melon pink, ½ skein
    - Orange, ¼ skein
    - Red-orange, ¼ skein
    - Red, ¼ skein
- Rubber cement or white glue

TOOLS

- Large-grit sandpaper
- Paintbrush
- Tape
- Hammer
- Needle-nose pliers
- Scissors

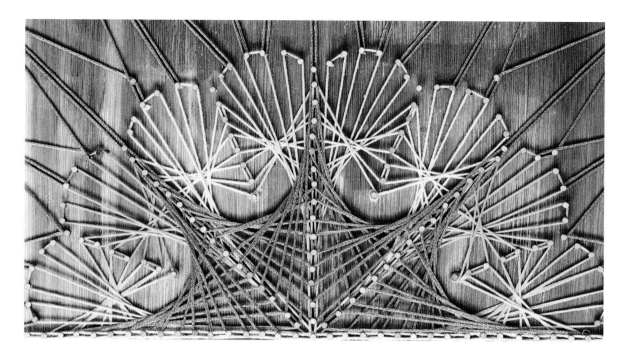

BOARD PREP

1. I painted my board with a blend of sunrise colors, focusing the darker purples toward the top where they will better set off the gold thread. Sand the edges of the board after the paint has dried, working the corners to give it a '70s vintage look.

2. Get the pattern from pages 108 to 110. Use carbon paper to transfer the lettering, using the instructions on page 23.

SUN RAYS

Tie gold thread onto #1. Wrap cc to #2-3-4-3-5-6-7-6-8-9-10-9-11-12-13-14-13-15-16-15-17-18-17-19-20-19-21-21a-21-22-23-22-24-25-24-26-27-26-28-29-28-30-31-30-32-33-32-34-35-34-36-37-36-38-39-40-39-41-42. Tie off.

CANARY YELLOW SUN SLICES

Tie canary yellow thread onto #43. Wrap cc to #44-45-46-47-48-49-50-51-52-53-54-55-56-57-58-59-60-61-4-62-63-64-65-2-66-41-67-68-69-70-40-71-72-73-74-75-76-77-78-79-80-81-82-83-84-85-86-87-88-89. Tie off.

LIGHT ORANGE SUN SLICES

Tie light orange thread onto #43. Wrap cc to #90-91-46-47-92-93-50-51-94-95-54-55-96-97-98-99-100-101-7-102-103-104-8-105-106-66-107-108-35-109-110-111-37-112-113-114-115-116-117-77-78-118-1-19-81-82-120-121-85-86-122-123-89. Tie off.

PALE YELLOW SUN SLICES

Tie pale yellow thread onto #124. Wrap cc to #90-91-125-126-92-93-127-128-94-95-129-130-96-97-131-14-100-101-132-12-103-104-133-134-66-135-136-109-110-31-137-112-113-29-138-116-117-139-140-1-18-119-141-142-120-121-143-144-122-123-145. Tie off.

MELON PINK SUN SLICES

Tie melon pink thread onto #124. Wrap cc to #146-147-125-126-148-149-127-128-150-151-129-130-152-153-154-16-155-156-18-20-157-158-159-160-66-161-162-158-157-23-25-156-155-27-163-153-152-139-140-151-150-141-142-149-148-143-144-147-146-145. Tie off.

GOLD SUNBURST

1. Tie gold thread onto #44. Wrap cc to #164-165-45-48-106-104-49-52-103-101-53-56-100-97-57-60-96-95-61-63-94-93-64-166-92-91-167-168, cl #10.

2. To form the second point, cc #169-170-91-92-171-158-93-94-157-156-95-96-155-153-97-100-152-151-101-103-150-149-104-106-148-147-165-164, cl #21a.

3. To form the third point, cc #172-173-147-148-107-109-149-150-110-112-151-152-113-116-153-155-117-118-156-157-119-120-158-171-121-122-170-169, cl #33.

4. To form the fourth point, cc #174-175-122-121-176-68-120-119-69-71-118-117-72-75-116-113-76-79-112-110-80-83-109-107-84-87-173-172-88. Tie off.

REFLECTION

1. Tie pale yellow thread onto #1.

2. Open outline across all nails between #1 and #44.

3. String single thread back across to #1, cc #177, string cl to #178, and back to #177. Tie off.

4. Tie melon pink thread onto #179. String cl to #180, back to #179, wrap cc to #181, across to #182, back to #181. Tie off.

5. Tie light orange thread onto #183. String cl to #184-183, cc #185, cl #186-185. Tie off.

6. Tie orange thread onto #187. String cl to #188-187, cc #189, cl #190-189, cc #191, cl #192-191. Tie off.

7. Tie red-orange thread onto #193. String cl to #194-193, cc #195, cl #196-195, cc #197, cl #198-197, cc #199, cl #200-199. Tie off.

8. Tie red thread onto #201. String cl to #202-201, cc #203, cl #204-203, cc #205, cl #206-205, cc #207, cl #208-207. Tie off.

9. Glue down all thread ends with glue or rubber cement.

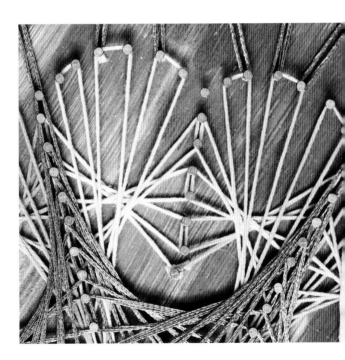

TROPICAL KISS

Flamingos are one of the few species on the planet that remain monogamous, choosing to frolic forever with their one-and-only. If you're lucky and so inclined, you can find a fellow human who carries the same attitude. Want to lock 'em in? Write a string art book and include the year of your first date in one of the patterns. Or just string your own sweet flamingo dedication with this project. This design inspires a lifetime of adoration . . . or at least a pair of margaritas.

THE LESSON

wrapping in the right direction

The direction in which the threads are wrapped around the nail can strongly impact the effect of the design. The devil is in the details for these two fraternizing flamingos.

For example, their feet would not be teardrop-shaped if the thread were wrapped in the wrong direction. Creating feetless flamingos seems a bit cruel—c'mon. The same method holds true for the typeface in this project, where skinny and wide portions help make the characters recognizable.

Notes: I've engineered this pattern so that each flamingo has the same start and finishing point to cut down on the annoying task of gluing the loose threads. A single thread will make up each flamingo. Wire brads are used because they have smaller heads, and so show a glitter of metal but don't distract from the color of the thread. Be careful to scoot thread down on the wire brad so that it is not at risk of slipping off. Also, don't make fun of the brads for having small heads.

MATERIALS

- Wooden board of choice, at least 12 x 8 ½ x ¾ in.
- Blue paint
- White paint
- 150 wire brads, 1-in. length
- Embroidery thread in the following colors:
    - Pink, 2 skeins
    - Canary yellow, 1 skein
- Rubber cement or white glue

TOOLS

- Large-grit sandpaper
- Wide paintbrush
- Tape
- Hammer
- Needle-nose pliers
- Scissors

BOARD PREP

1. Paint the board with two layers of blue paint.

2. While the second layer of blue paint is still wet, brush white paint in from the top, fading the white into the blue. With a dusting motion, use a wide brush to gradually blend the white with the blue.

3. Sand the edges and front corners of the board to create a well-worn look.

4. Get the pattern from page 115 and tape it to the board.

5. Tack the dots with a nail to mark the pattern, or drive all nails in about halfway and work with the pattern in place.

START THE WING

1. Tie pink thread on at nail #1 and wrap cl to #2-3-4-5. This will get us into position to start working around the wing.

2. Continue working cl to #23-4-22-3-21-2-20-26-19-25-18-24-17-23-16-22-15-21-14-20-13-19-12-18-11-17-10-16-9-15-8-14-7-13-6-12-5-11.

OUTLINE WING

Work the thread so that it wraps around the outside edge of the wing by wrapping cl to #12-13-14-15-16-17-18-19.

WORK UP THE NECK

Wrap cl to #38-20-39-33-40-34-41-35-42-36-43-37-44.

BRIDGE TO UPPER NECK

Continue wrapping to #47-43-46-42-45.

UPPER NECK

Continue wrapping to #51-46-52-47-53-48-54-49-55-50-56-51-57-52-57.

HEAD

The head is a circular spray of thread that gives the impression of an eye toward the center. Work around without skipping nails as follows: #65-58-66-59-67-60-68-61-69-62-54-63-53-64-55-65-56-66-57-67-58-67-59-68-60.

BEAK

Continue to #70-71-72-62.

COMPLETE THE HEAD AND NECK

1. Wrap around outside of nails #62 to #52 all at once (not around each individual nail). Wrap cl around #52.

2. Wrap around outside of nails #52 to #45 all at once. Wrap cl around #45.

3. Wrap each of the following nails cc so that thread is on the left side of the neck: #44-43-42-41-40.

4. Wrap nails #40 to 36 all at once, with thread on left side of the nails.

BELLY

1. Wrap each nail #36-35-34-33-21.

2. Open outline from #21-27-28-29-30.

LEGS

1. You will work down the legs and back up along the same strings to create very skinny legs. Wrap cl around #73-74, cc #73. Move along the same thread back up to #30.

2. Open outline #30-31-32-1. Wrap cl around #75-76-77, cc #76-75-1. Tie off and glue down the thread end.

SECOND FLAMINGO

Repeat these instructions for the second flamingo, using the same methods and reasoning. Keep in mind that you'll need to wrap in the opposite direction on some nails to achieve the mirror image. If you'd like the second flamingo to look a bit different (bulkier or thinner in places), wrap in the same direction as the instructions for the first flamingo.

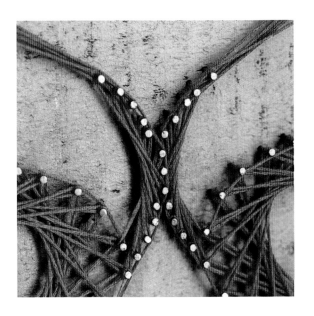

"ESTABLISHED" TYPE

1. Use the numbers provided in the pattern, or select the geometric font in the Appendix (pages 120 to 121). Use your own "established" date, two names, or simply the word "Love."

2. With canary yellow thread, experiment with backstitching and wrapping in various directions to create thin and thick lines for each character.

PARROT HEAD

My first string art project was a parrot produced by Open Door Enterprises and designed by John Eichinger. At nine years of age, I was undeterred by the "ages 10 and older" advisory and really trying to kick a serious Super Mario Bros 3 habit.

I happily applied the black fabric and pins and lost half of the string, but somehow managed to finish before the summer was out. Sharing my own parrot string art design is my little way of coming full-circle, and I hope you are equally inspired.

THE LESSON

adding colors in order

When you venture into creating your own patterns (and I know you will), be mindful of the order in which you string—some colors will need to get on the board before others so that your layering looks right. The feathers of our bird are a good exercise in stringing layers of color in the right order.

MATERIALS

- Wooden board of choice, at least 12 x 12 x ¾ in.
- Blue paint
- Green paint
- Carbon paper or pencil
- White paint
- Black paint
- About 260 nails, ½-in. length (one 1.75 oz package)
- Embroidery thread in the following colors:
  - Brown, ¼ skein
  - Satin blue, ½ skein
  - Satin green, ½ skein
  - Satin yellow, ½ skein
  - Satin red, 1 skein
  - Orange, ¼ skein
  - Purple, ¼ skein
  - Pink, ¼ skein
- Rubber cement or white glue

TOOLS

- Large-grit sandpaper
- Paintbrush
- Tape
- Hammer
- Needle-nose pliers
- Scissors

BOARD PREP

1. Paint the face and edges of the board blue.

2. Blend in green paint on the edges of the face.

3. Let dry and sand the edges of the board to distress the look of the blue and green paint.

4. Get the pattern from pages 116 to 119. Transfer the painted parts of the pattern via the instructions on page 23. Paint the parrot's face area white. Let dry. Paint the eye and "eyelash" feathers black.

BRANCHES

1. Tie brown thread onto #1. String cc to #2-3-2-4-2-1. Tie off.

2. Tie onto #5. String cl to #6-7-8-7-6-5. Tie off.

3. Tie onto #9. String cl to #10-11-12-13-14-13-15-13-12-11-10-16-10-9. Tie off.

4. Tie onto #17. String cl to #18-19-18-17. Tie off.

5. Tie onto #20. String cc to #21-22-23-24-25-24-23-26-23-22-21-27-28-29-30-31-30-29-28-27-21-20. Tie off.

BLUE FEATHERS

1. Tie blue satin thread onto #34. Wrap cl to #35, cc #34, cl #36, cc #34, cl #37-36-35-36-37-38.

2. Wrap cc #39-40-77-41-42.

3. Wrap cl #43-41-43-40-43-39-43-38-43-37-43-44-36-1.

4. Wrap cc #45-46-47-48-49-50-51-52-53-54, cl #55-135.

5. Wrap cc #52-53-135-54-55-42-56-58-56-57-58-59-58-60-59-61-60-61-62-61-62-63-62-63-64-65-62-65-66-65-66-64-67-66-67-68-67-68-69-67-70-69-70-71-70-71-72-71-72-5-72-5-73-5-73. Tie off.

GREEN FEATHERS

1. Tie green satin thread onto #74. Wrap cc to #75-35-75-34-74-76-34-75-74. Tie off.

2. Tie onto #77. Wrap cl to #41-77-41-78-42-41-42-57-42-57, cc #78.

3. Wrap cl #59-57-59-79-59-80-79-80-81-82-59-63-82-63.

4. Wrap cc #81-64-63-64-83-81-84-85-83-64-85-86-64-86-68-86-68.

5. Wrap cl #85-69-68-69-87-69-87-88-69-73-69, cc #73-88.

6. Wrap cl #89-73-89-90-89-90-91-90-91-92-91-92. Tie off.

YELLOW ON HIDDEN WING

Tie yellow satin thread onto #75. Wrap cl to #135, cc #74-136-137, cl #74-135-136-135-75. Tie off.

RED SHOULDER

Tie red satin thread onto #219. Wrap cl to #229-226-230-227-225-230-225-229-230-196-175-219. Tie off.

ORANGE BEAK

1. Tie orange thread onto #175. Freeform fill the beak, ending back at #175.

2. Open outline #175-176-175-176. Repeat open outline pattern around the beak, ending again at #175. Tie off.

RED HEAD AND NECK FEATHERS

1. Tie red satin thread onto #177. Wrap cl to #178-184-179-178-179-177-184-180-179.

2. Wrap cc #185-184-180-179-182-180-186-185-181-183-182-188-183-191-192-188-189-193-194-189-191-195-196-197-198-199-200-201-187-186. Tie off.

YELLOW WING FEATHERS

1. Tie yellow satin thread onto #40. Wrap cl to #138-77-40-78-77-78, cc #138.

2. Wrap cl #80-78-80-81-80-81-138-140-139-140-81-139, cc #141, cl #81-84.

3. Wrap cc #141-142-143-144-145-144-145-144-145.

4. Wrap cc #146-145-146-147-146-147-85-84-85-147.

5. Wrap cl #143-148-149-148-149-87-147-87-88-87-88-149-151-150-151-88-151, cc #153.

6. Wrap cl #149-148-153-143-152-153-152-17-153-9-17-154-9-155-154-156-155-156-92-156-92-151-92-17-20-17-157-20-158-159.

7. Wrap cc #157-160-161-162-163-164-165-40-159-20-152-166-152-167-166-167-143-167-142-144-142-168-167-168-141-169-168-169-138-169-138-40. Tie off.

RED BODY AND WING

1. Tie red satin thread around #202. Wrap cc #203-204-136-205-135-205-202-204-196-206-207-193-192-207-208-210-211-191-211-204-211-204-196.

2. Wrap cl #212, cc#209-208-212-208-207-212.

3. Wrap cl #214-204-215-214-216-215-216, cc #38.

4. Wrap cl #217-218-38-76-216-212-38-37-76-216-76-37-38-39-40-39.

5. Wrap cc #219-221-224-222-223-225-226-223-161-227-228-162-219-222-40-231-223-231, wrap left of #223 to #222-223, wrap left of #222 to #219-228-227-228-226-227-225-226-224-225-221-224-164-221-220-163-220-221, wrap right of #220 to #232-220, wrap right of #232 to #20-232-157-20-160-157-163-160-164-163-159-164-158-159-161-158-162-161-165-162-40-165. Tie off.

PURPLE HEAD FEATHERS

Tie purple thread onto #183. Wrap cl to #233-183-234-183-235-183-236-183. Tie off.

SMALL LEAVES

1. Tie green satin thread onto #30. Wrap cl to #93-97-96-95-94-93-30-93-95-93-97-95-97-98-97-98-94-98-96-94-30-96-30. Tie off.

2. Tie onto #25. Wrap cl around #99-100-101-102-25-101-25-99-101-102-99. Continue cc to #102-100-102-25-100-25. Tie off.

LARGE LEAF BUNCH

1. Tie onto #7. Wrap cc to #104-106-107-104-108-109-104-110-111-104-105-7-103. Open outline around leaf back to #7.

2. Wrap cc to #113-114-115-116-117-118-119-120-121-122-7-122. Open outline back around to #7.

3. Wrap cc to #7-118-123-124-119-115-125-126-127-128-129-130-123-124-131-132-125-126-133-134-129-133. Open outline around leaf back to #7. Tie off.

PINK FLOWERS

1. Tie pink thread onto #237. Wrap cl to #238-239-22-240-241-242-243-237-22-242-238-240-243-239-241-237. Tie off.

2. Tie onto #249. Wrap cl to #250-249-251-249-252-249-253-254-251-255-252-256-250-257-253-255-250-254-252-257-251-256-253-249. Tie off.

3. Tie onto #244. Wrap cl to #245-244-246-244-247-244-248-244. Tie off. Repeat this step for the other two X-shaped flowers.

TAIL FEATHER ACCENT COLORS

1. Tie green satin thread onto #171. Wrap cc to #45-46-47-171. Tie off. Tie green satin thread onto #170. Wrap cc to #54-53-52-170. Tie off.

2. Tie yellow satin thread onto #173. Wrap cc to #46-47-173-48-49-50-51-172-52-53-172. Tie off.

3. Tie red satin thread onto #43. Wrap cc to #47-48-43-49-50-174-51-52-174. Tie off. Glue down the thread ends on the piece using glue or rubber cement.

OCTOPUS'S GARDEN

Earth's oceans are so vast and mysterious that our knowledge of the moon is far more detailed. Twenty thousand leagues under the sea, creatures stranger than fiction roam the sands—with many alienlike organisms yet to be discovered. Here, we've imagined a glimpse into an undersea gathering, where an octopus emerges from the depths as our host.

THE LESSON

combining methods

This is the most advanced project in the book; it combines artistic methods and stringing patterns from previous projects. We are working with a few new styles of parabolic angles on the fish, but the fundamental ideas are the same as the parabolic shapes you have strung before. Take note that even with simple shapes such as fish, there are more than a few ways to complete the look of bodies and fins.

The color palette in this piece is very deliberate, with dark purple muting the looming octopus while brighter colors put the smaller marine life center stage. Hot colors and cool colors are spaced methodically throughout to maintain balance and keep the eye moving. Consider how color choices will affect the result of your own designs.

MATERIALS

- Wooden board of choice, at least 10 ¾ x 17 x ¾ in.
- Black paint
- White paint
- Purple paint
- Blue paint
- About 300 nails, ½-in. length (2 1.5oz packages)
- Embroidery thread in the following colors:
  - Purple, 1 skein
  - Silver, ½ skein
  - Blue, ½ skein
  - Light blue, ½ skein
  - Yellow, ½ skein
  - Orange, ½ skein
  - Light purple, ½ skein
  - Lavender, ½ skein
  - Red, ½ skein
  - Pink, ½ skein
  - Orange-yellow, ½ skein
  - Sandy yellow, ½ skein
  - Lime green, ½ skein
  - Forest green, ½ skein
- Rubber cement or white glue

TOOLS

- Large-grit sandpaper
- Paintbrush
- Tape
- Hammer
- Needle-nose pliers
- Scissors

BOARD PREP

1. Paint board with black paint, making sure to paint the sides of the board, too.

2. While the black paint is still wet, streak the front of the board with white, purple, and blue paint to imitate deep sea waves.

3. Get the pattern from pages 111 to 113.

HEAD AND LEFT TENTACLES

1. Tie purple thread onto #1. Open outline by wrapping cl from #1-2-1-3-2-4-3-5-4. Repeat this pattern of wrapping all the way around the octopus head to #6. This wrapping style will give dimension to the rounded corners of the eyes and head.

2. Continue the open outline on each nail from #6 to #7, then to #8. Continue open outline around the small tentacle to #9.

3. Zigzag outline down the tentacle to #11. Zigzag back to #10. Open outline on each nail back up to #9.

4. Open outline from #9-8-9-7-8-7.

5. Zigzag outline from #7 to #12. Zigzag from #12 to #13, then open outline back up to #12.

6. Zigzag outline from #12 to #14. Open outline back up to #12.

7. Open outline from #12 to #7. Tie off.

MIDDLE TENTACLES

1. Tie purple thread onto #15. Zigzag outline on each nail to #16, continue to #17, then on to #18. Open outline from #18 to #17.

2. Zigzag outline each nail from #17 to #19. Zigzag outline from #19 to #20. Open outline from #20 back up to #19.

3. Zigzag outline each nail from #19 to #17. Open outline from #17 to #16.

4. Zigzag outline from #16 to #19. Open outline from #19 up to #15. Tie off.

5. Tie purple thread onto #21. Zigzag outline on each nail to #22.

6. Continue zigzag outline from #22 to #23.

7. Zigzag outline from #23 back to #22. Continue zigzag back up to #24.

8. Zigzag from #24 to #25.

9. Zigzag from #25 to #26, then back up to #21. Tie off.

10. Tie purple thread onto #27. Zigzag outline to #28-30-29.

11. Zigzag outline back up to #28.

12. Zigzag outline from #28 to #31.

13. Zigzag from #31 to #30.

14. Zigzag back up to #31; continue up to #32.

15. Zigzag from #32 to #31; continue to #28. Tie off.

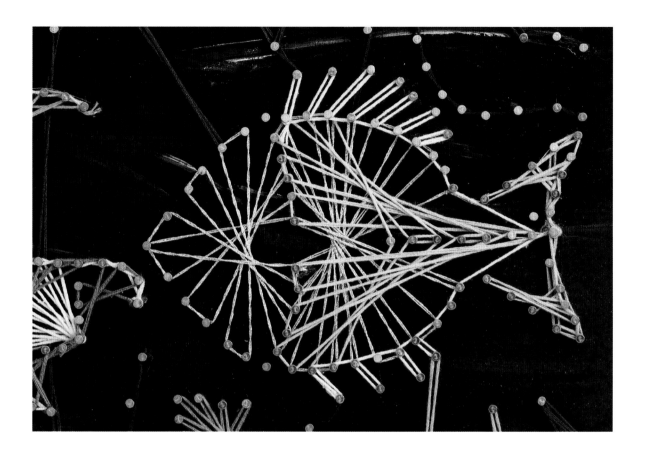

RIGHT SIDE TENTACLES

1. Tie purple thread onto #4. Zigzag on each nail from #4 to #33 and on to #34, then back up to #33.

2. Zigzag outline from #33 to #35, then back up to #33.

3. Zigzag outline from #33 to #4.

4. Zigzag outline from #4 to #36, then back up to #37.

5. Open outline from #37 all the way around the small tentacle to #39.

6. Zigzag outline from #39 to #4. Tie off.

SMALL TENTACLE PIECES AT THE BOTTOM

1. Tie purple thread onto #40. Zigzag outline from #40 to #41 and back. Tie off.

2. Tie onto #42. Open outline, wrapping cl around each nail as shown in pattern to #48. Tie off.

3. Tie on to #49. Zigzag outline on each nail to #50. Open outline back up to #49. Tie off.

4. Tie on to #51. Open outline cl on #52-51-53-52. Continue open outline pattern to #54. Zigzag back around the tentacle to #51. Tie off.

PONYFISH SILVER BODY

1. Tie silver thread onto #55. Wrap cc onto #56-57-58-59-60-61-62-63-64-65-66-67-34-68-69-70-71-72-73-74-75-76-77-78-79.

2. Wrap from #79 to #80. Continue to #81-82-78-77-83-84-74-73-85-86-87-26-88-61-89-90-60-57-91-81-56. Tie off.

PONYFISH BLUE BODY AND BACK FIN

1. Tie blue thread onto #92. Wrap cc to #80-78-93-94-77-74-95-96-73-70-97-98-69-34-99-67-65-98-97-64-88-96-95-61-60-94-93-57-56-92.

2. String from #92 to #100. Open outline fin: #105-100-101-106-101-102-107-102-103-108-103-104-105-104.

3. Zigzag outline on each nail from #104 up to #100. String to #109.

4. Open outline fin: #109-114-109-110-115-110-111-116-111-112-117-112-113-112.

5. Zigzag outline from #112 to #109. String to #92. Tie off.

PONYFISH TOP AND BOTTOM FINS

Tie light blue thread onto #118. Wrap cl to #65-118-65-67-68-119-68-71-72-120-72-75-121-75-76-122-79-93-55-123-58-59-124-59-62-125-62-63-126-63-66-127-66-34-128-34-69-129-69-70-29-70. Tie off.

FIRST GOLDFISH

1. Tie yellow thread onto #130. Wrap cl to #131-130-132-130-133-130-134-130-135-130-136-130-137-130-138-130-139-130.

2. Tie orange thread onto #140. Wrap cl to #141-142-143-144-145-130-146-147-136-137-131-132-138-139-133-134-139-148-149-130-150-151-152-153-154-155. Tie off.

SECOND GOLDFISH

1. Tie yellow thread onto #156. Wrap cl to #157-156-158-156-159-156-160-156-161-156-162-156-163-156.

2. Tie orange thread onto #164. Wrap cl onto #165-166-167-168-169-156-170-171-161-162-157-158-163-172-159-160-173-156-174-175-176-177-178-179. Tie off.

THIRD GOLDFISH

Tie orange thread onto #180. Wrap cl to #181-180-182-180-183-180-184-180-185-180-186-180-187-180. Tie off.

ANGELFISH

1. Tie silver thread on to #189. Wrap cl around each nail in numerical order from #189 to #207. Tie off.

2. Tie light purple thread onto #197. Wrap cc to #200-202-208-209-204-206-210-211-212-213-214-215-216-215-217-214-218-219-211-210-190-192-209-208-194-220-197. Tie off.

3. Tie lavender thread onto #217. Wrap cc to #221-200-217-218-202-204-219-190-206-212-192-194-213-216-220-222-216-215-217. Tie off.

TANG

1. Tie red thread onto #223. Wrap cc around each nail in numerical order from #223 to #237. Tie off.

2. Tie silver thread onto #238. Wrap cl to #225-224-238-239-240-241-242-243-244-245-246-236-247. Tie off.

PINK CORAL

Tie pink thread onto #248. Wrap cc to next nail, then back to #248 to complete an open outline. Continue open outline from #248 to #249.

ORANGE CORAL

Tie orange-yellow thread onto #275. Open outline to #23-276-277-278-279-280-281-282-264-20-283-262. Tie off.

STARFISH

Tie sandy yellow onto #48. Wrap cl, creating an open outline on the following pattern: #250-48-251-48-251-252-251-252-250-252-253-252-253-254-253-254-250-254-255-254-255-256-255-256-250-256-257-256-257-258-257-258-250-258-259-258-259-260-259-260-250-260-261-260-261-262-261-262-250-262-263-262-263-250-263-264-263-264-265-264-265-250-265-266-265-266-267-266-267-250-267-268-267-268-48-268-48. Tie off.

SEAWEED

1. Tie lime green thread onto #250. Wrap cl around #251-252-253-254-253-121-253-248-255-256-255-252-248-252-250-252-250. Tie off.

2. Tie lime green thread onto #257. Wrap cl around #258, then open outline to #259, coming back to #258. Repeat on other side, creating an open outline between #258 and #260. Continue this pattern of single outline for the stem and open outline for the leaves. Tie off at #261.

3. Tie forest green thread on to #257. Wrap cl around #262-263-257-264-265-263-266-265-267-268-269-270. Open outline to #42. Open outline #270-271-268-265-263-257.

4. Tie forest green thread on to #272. Wrap cl around #274-227-273-227-272. Tie off.

TINY FISH

1. Tie red thread onto #284. Open outline to #287-284-285-286-287-288-289-287-284. Tie off.

2. Tie red thread onto #290. Repeat pattern from the first tiny fish. Tie off at #290.

3. Tie red thread onto #291. Open stitch around the three nails, returning to #291. Tie off.

4. Tie pink thread onto #292. Open stitch around #293-294-295-296-293-297-292. Tie off. Glue down all the thread ends with glue or rubber cement.

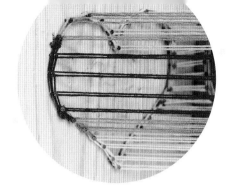

3-D HEARTS

Though they are the most simple of shapes, hearts often carry a big meaning. That symbolism is universal, and it is for *everyone* to enjoy. I hope you get to know many hearts in your life, and that you have the opportunity to give yours away.

a new dimension

String art can be expanded from the traditional 2-D platform to create mobiles, frames, and sculptures. This simple 3-D representation is a very basic shape to get you started on a path to multi-dimensional string art creations.

MATERIALS

- 2 wooden boards of choice, each at least 5 x 5 x 1 in.
- 70 nails, ½-in. length
- 4 nails, 1 ½-in. length
- Embroidery thread in the following colors:
  - Purple, ¼ skein
  - Blue, ¼ skein
  - Green, ¼ skein
  - Yellow, ¼ skein
  - Orange, ¼ skein
  - Red, ¼ skein
- Rubber cement or white glue

TOOLS

- Large-grit sandpaper
- Tape
- Hammer
- Needle-nose pliers
- Scissors

BOARD PREP

Sand the edges of each board. Set boards at a 90° angle; using the 1-inch nails, nail the back of one board into the side of the other to make an L shape.

SETTING THE PATTERN

1. The heart patterns for this project are designed so that the nails farthest from the viewer are closer together. This allows for the colors in the corner to be bolder and more easily seen through the larger spaces of the strings in front of it. Tape the heart patterns from page 122 into place on each board, making sure that the nail dots that are closer together are in the corner. You will want the hearts to be exact mirrors of each other, so use a ruler if you aren't sure if they are on straight.

2. After you've set the nails, use a pair of pliers to gently tip each nail away from the corner. This slight bend will help to hold the string behind the head of the nail.

STRINGING THE HEART

The color choices for your heart can vary, but be advised that standard rainbow colors really punch up the 3-D aspect of this project. Work from the purple thread out to the red thread. Simply follow the colored dots on the pattern to create the same rainbow that I did. Tie purple thread onto #1. Wrap cl around #2, then back to #1. String to #3. Repeat this sequence to complete each section of the heart. Wrap the string tightly around each nail as you work.

APPENDIX

BASIC SHAPES FOR PIECING

Create your own geometric string art pictorials with these basic shapes. Combine, resize, and multiply these to create flowers, birds, fish, and more.

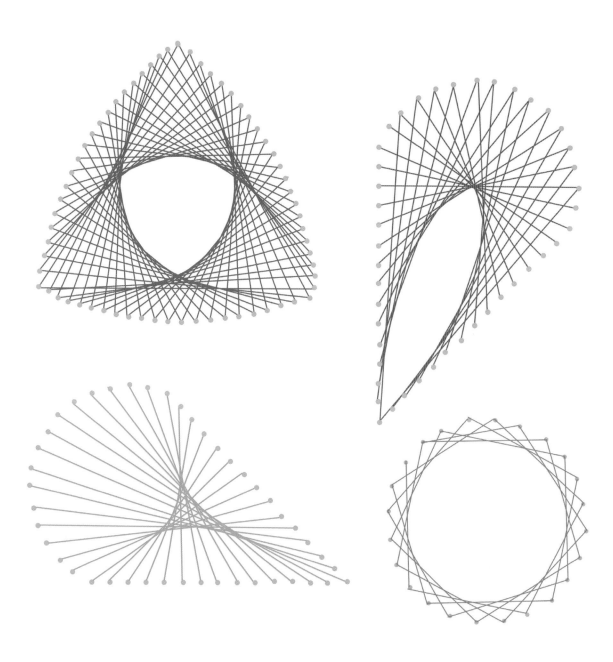

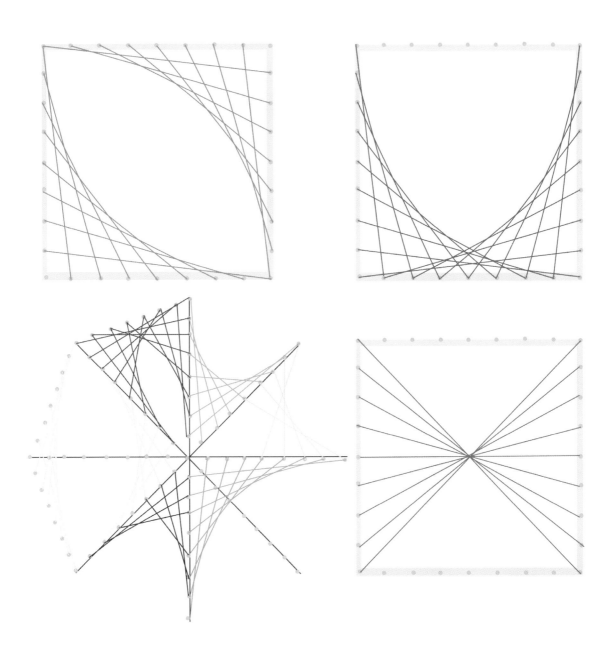

EXAMPLES OF GEOMETRIC STRING ART SHAPES

Complex geometric string art designs are often just layers of the same simple geometric shapes. Here are a few examples of how you can stack sets of parabolic angles to create intricate designs.

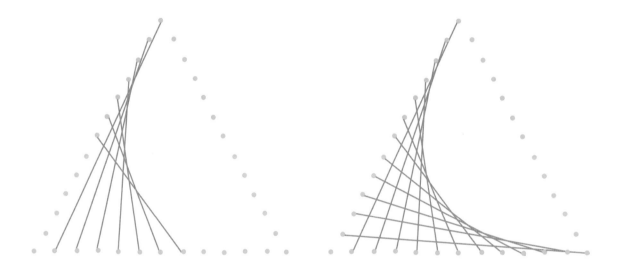

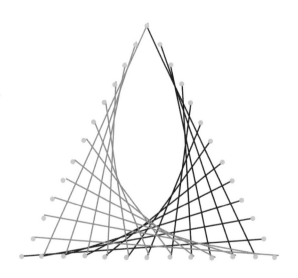

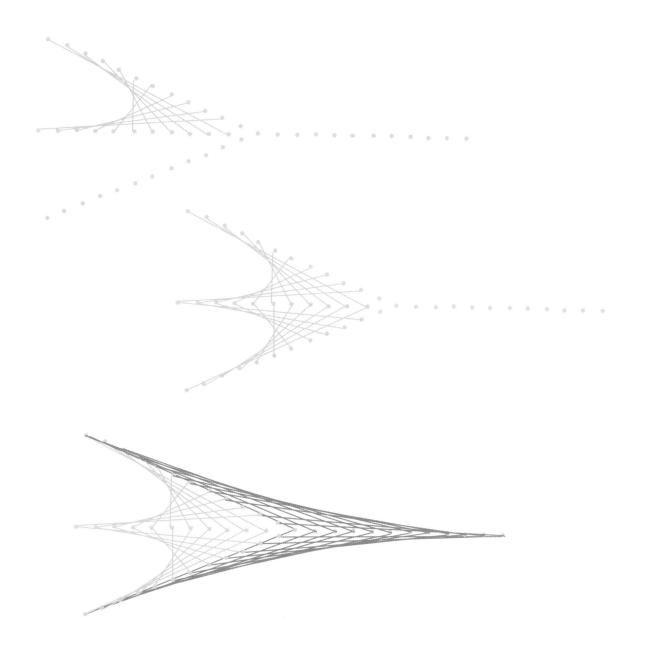

PLOTTING POINTS TO CREATE CIRCULAR PATTERNS

There are several circular string art patterns in this book, but you may want to create a circle of a certain size that I haven't included here. To create a perfect circle, employ an old-fashioned compass.

CREATING THE CIRCLE

For example, if you are trying to create a 10-inch circle, measure 5 inches away from the point of the compass, then set the compass pencil at the 5-inch mark. Circle around to create a full 10-inch circle. Those instructions may seem obvious, but really, when is the last time you saw someone bust out a compass?

CREATING EVENLY SPACED DOTS AROUND THE CIRCUMFERENCE

But how do you create an even set of dots all around the circle? First find the circumference of the circle.

This formula is $C = 2\pi r$, where "r" is the radius of the circle, and we are finding "C," the circumference.

Stay with me, now, this is easy stuff, even for me (or dare I say, easy as . . . pi?). This formula is 3.14 multiplied by the radius of the circle (that's 5 inches in our example), multiplied by 2.

For our example, the formula would be $C = 2 * 3.14 * 5$. The circumference of our 10-inch circle is 31.42 inches.

How many points do you want on the circle? The more points, the more intricate your design will be. Divide the circumference by the number of points you'd like. This number is how far apart the points on your circle will be.

Make a mark on the circle with a pencil, and then use another artifact—a divider—to measure the distance between each point. This tool is similar to a compass, except the two arms are both points. Use a ruler to adjust the divider so that the arms are as far apart as your dots need to be.

Touch one point of the divider to the mark you made on the circle, then touch the other divider point to the circle's edge and mark there with a pencil. You've now got two marks.

Lift up the first point of the divider and pivot it around to the edge of the circle. Mark again. You can use a ruler to measure between points, but the divider is much more accurate and kind of fun to walk around the circle.

PATTERNS

Copy patterns at enlargement percentages shown.

If a pattern spans multiple pages, first copy, then trim around pattern pieces and cut alongside the crosshairs. Position pieces on a window, or even a bright TV or computer monitor. Align crosshairs and tape the pattern pieces together.

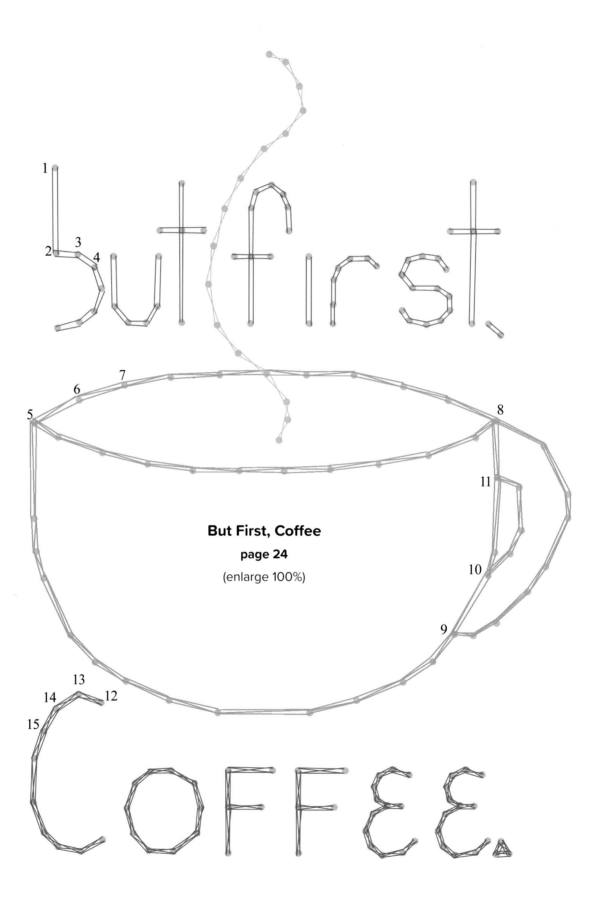

But First, Coffee

page 24

(enlarge 100%)

State Scrapbook

page 28

(enlarge 100%)

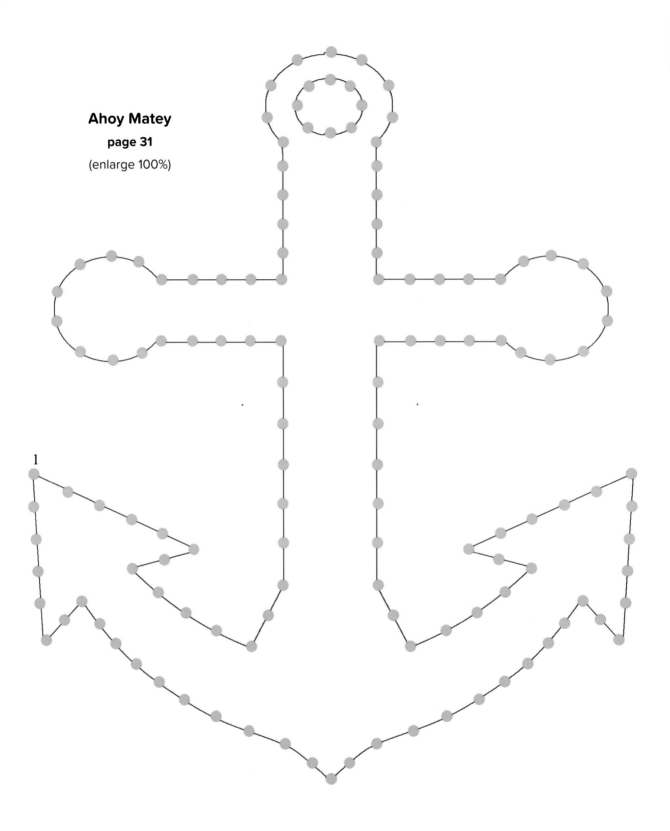

Ahoy Matey

page 31

(enlarge 100%)

1

Rainbow Mandala

page 34

(enlarge 100%)

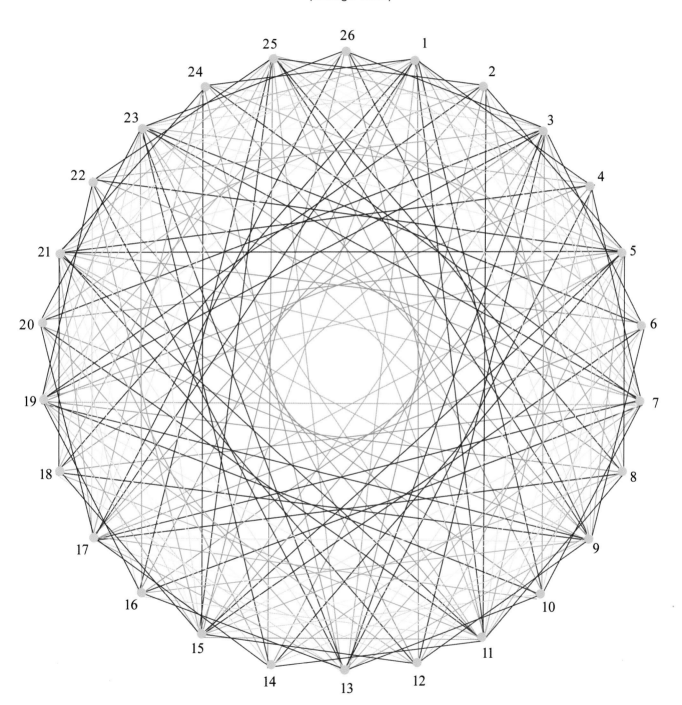

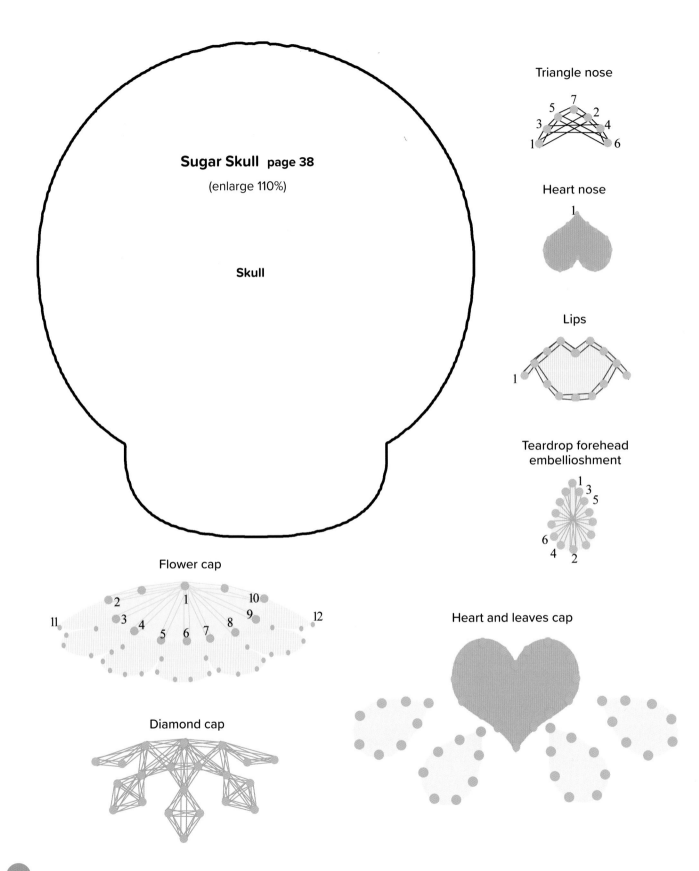

Sugar Skull page 38

(enlarge 110%)

Skull

Triangle nose

Heart nose

Lips

Teardrop forehead
embellioshment

Flower cap

Diamond cap

Heart and leaves cap

Mandala eyes

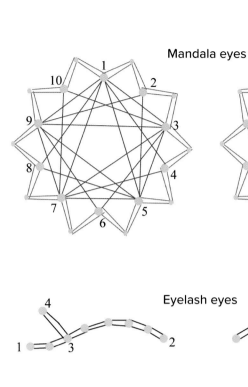

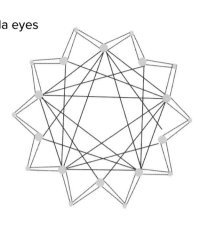

Green leaves embellishment

Eyelash eyes

X spots

Diamond eyes

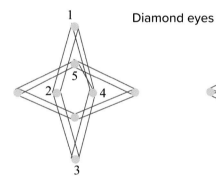

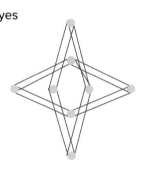

Teeth

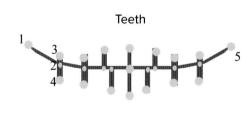

Triangle eyes

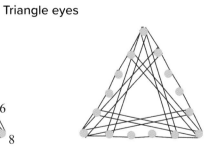

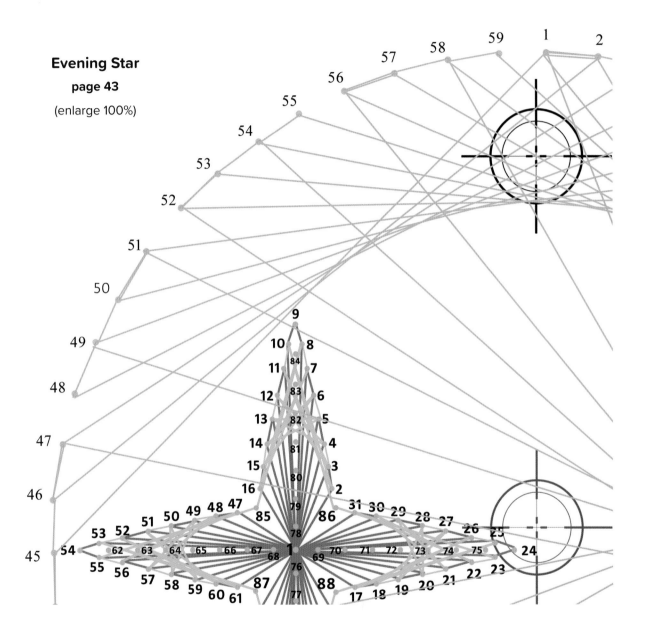

Evening Star

page 43

(enlarge 100%)

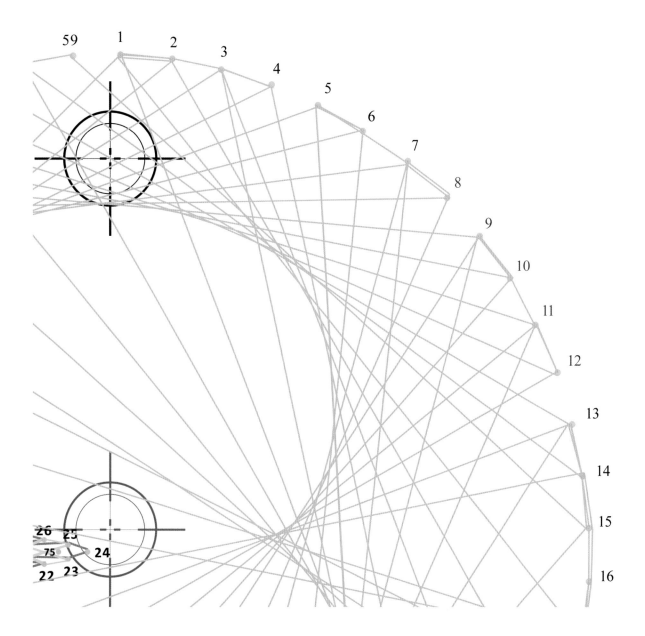

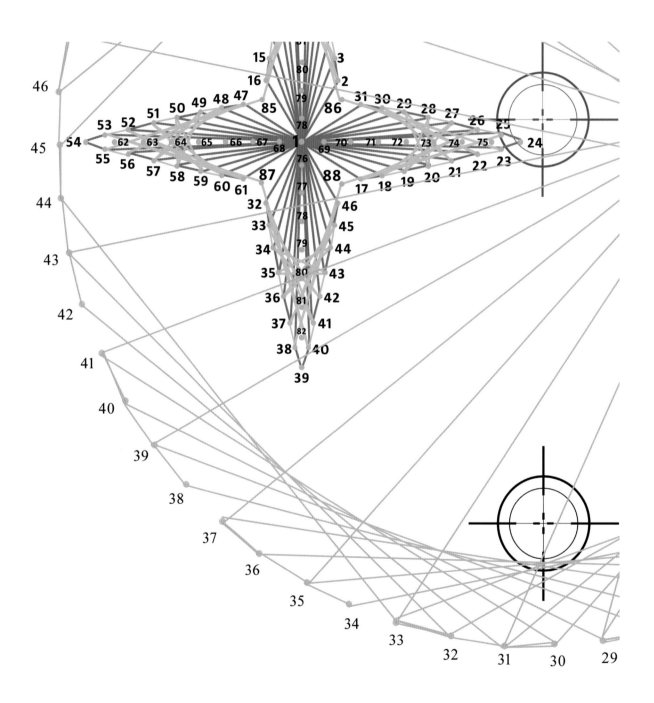

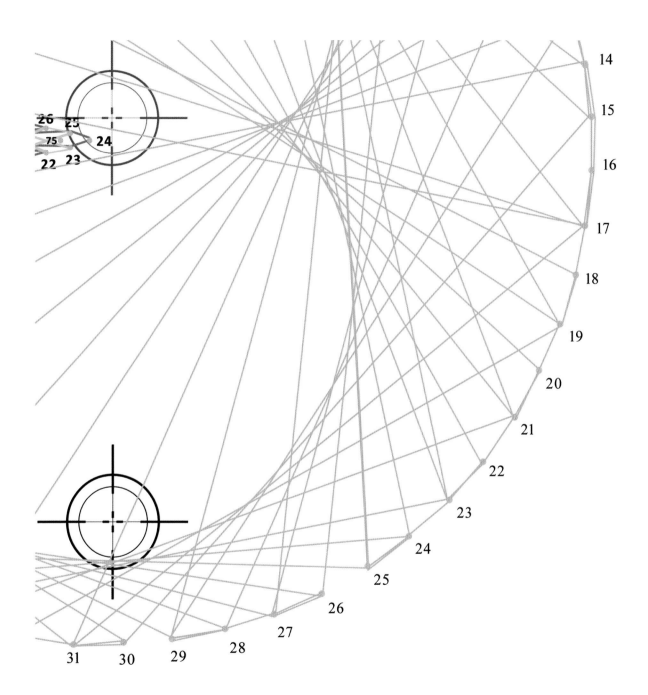

14

15

16

17

18

19

20

21

22

23

24

25

26

27

28

29

30

31

26 25
75 24
22 23

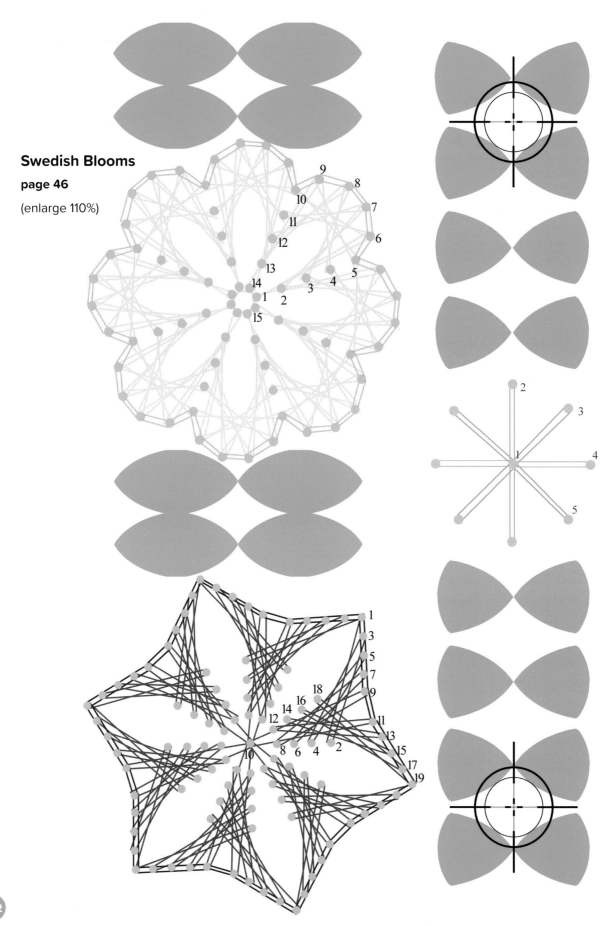

Swedish Blooms
page 46

(enlarge 110%)

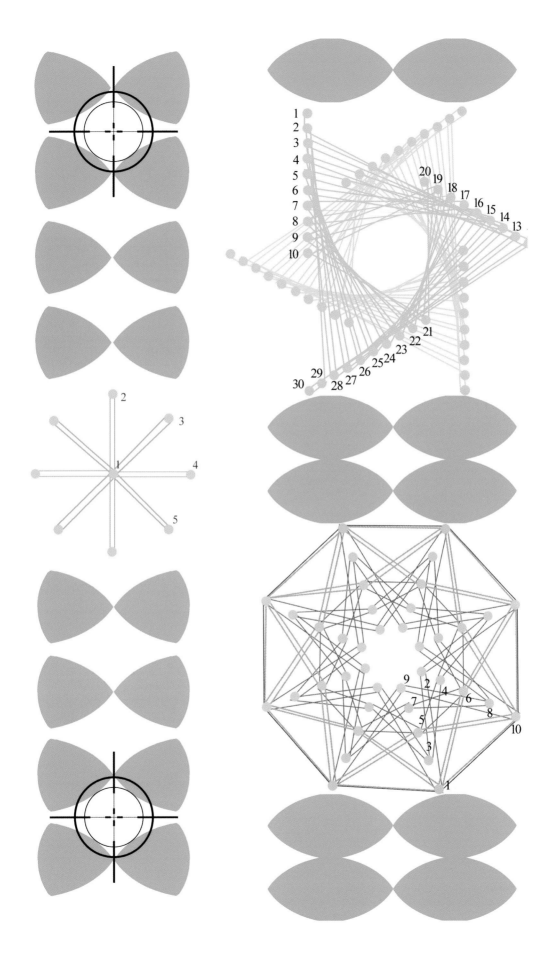

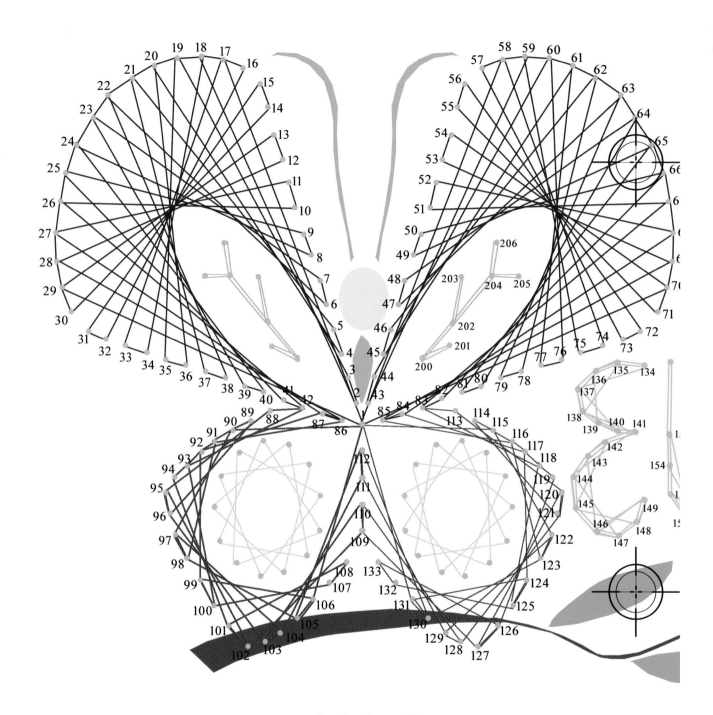

Lucky Butterfly

page 53

(enlarge 110%)

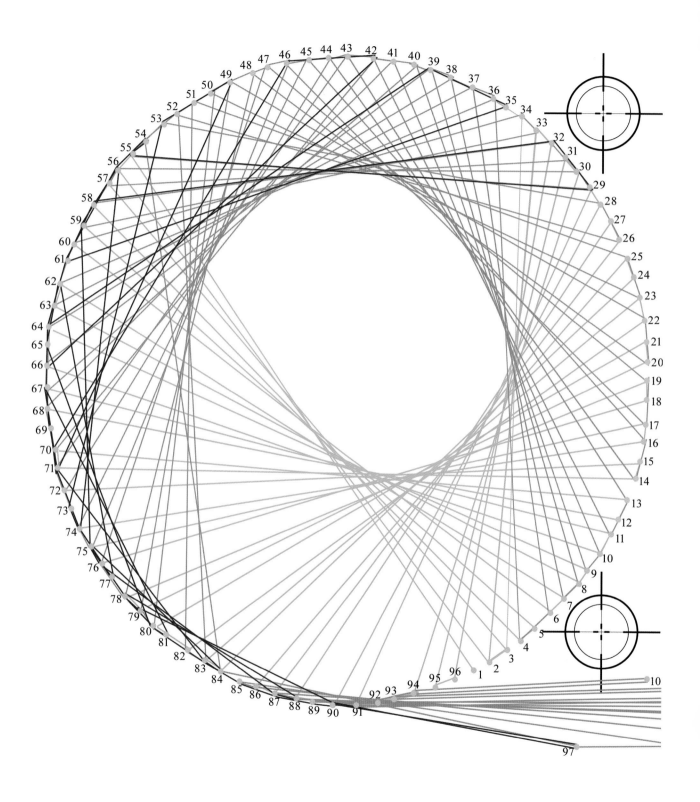

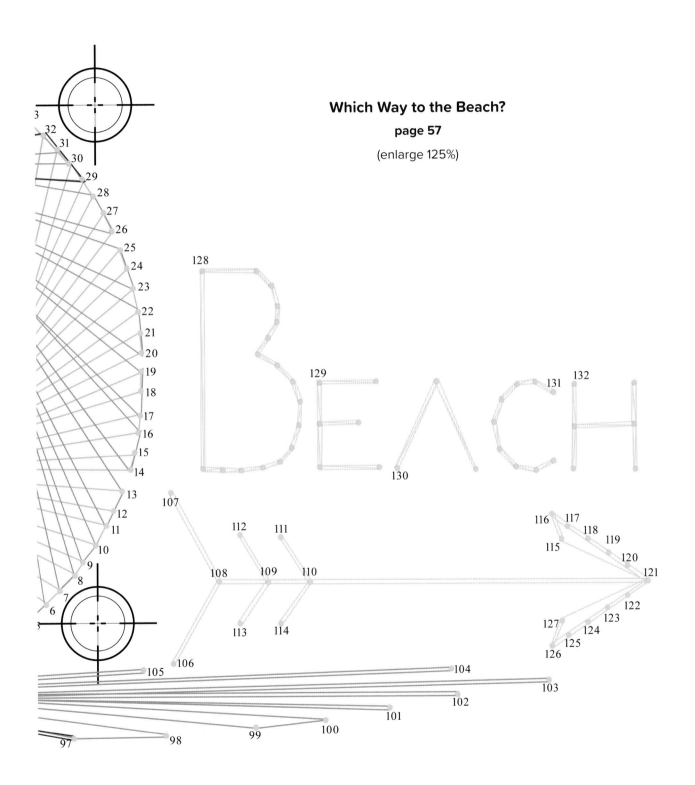

Which Way to the Beach?

page 57

(enlarge 125%)

Here Comes the Sun

page 60

(enlarge 125%)

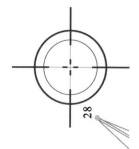

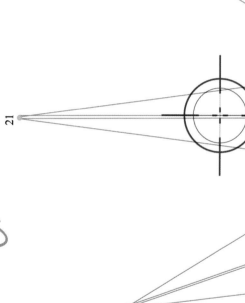

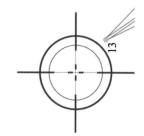

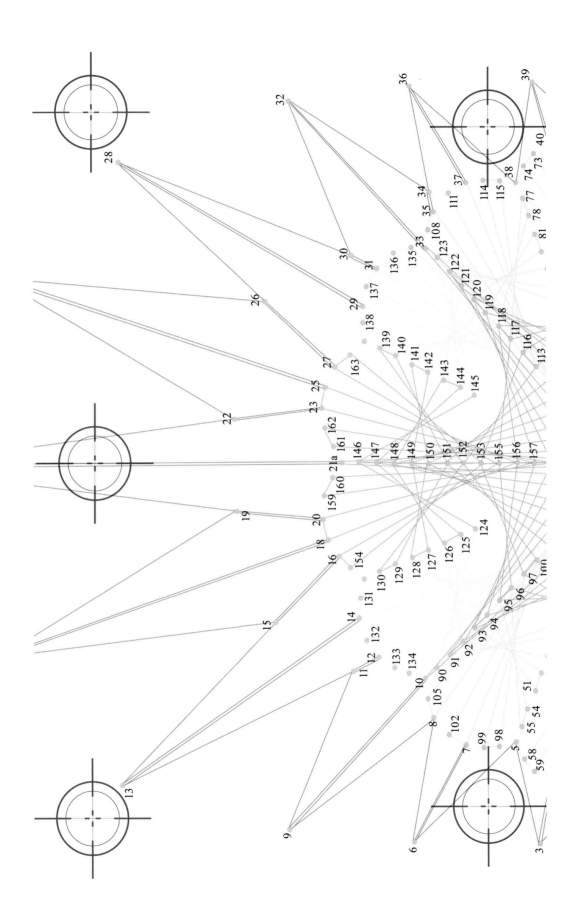

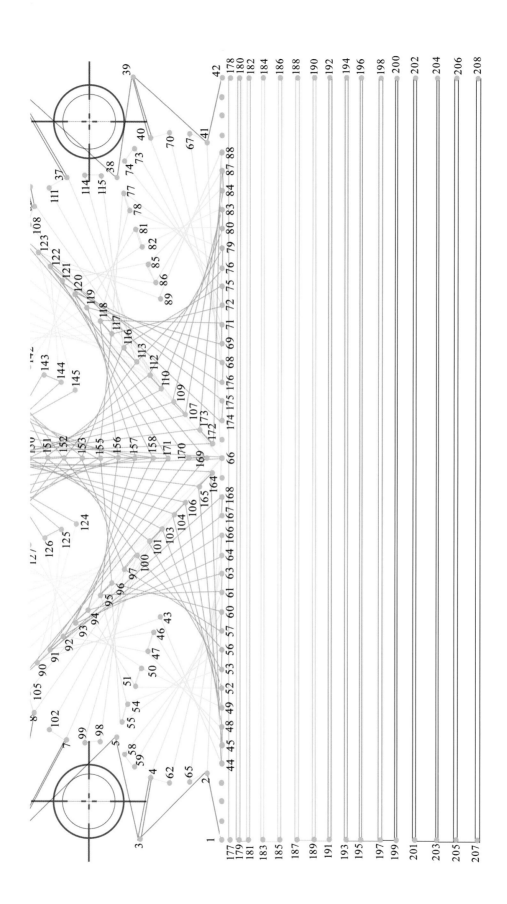

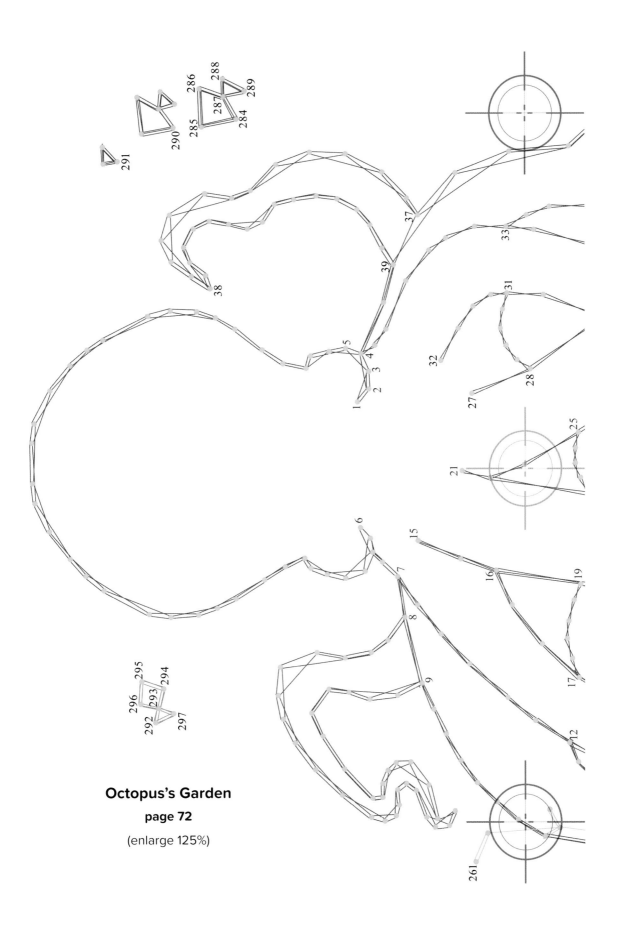

Octopus's Garden

page 72

(enlarge 125%)

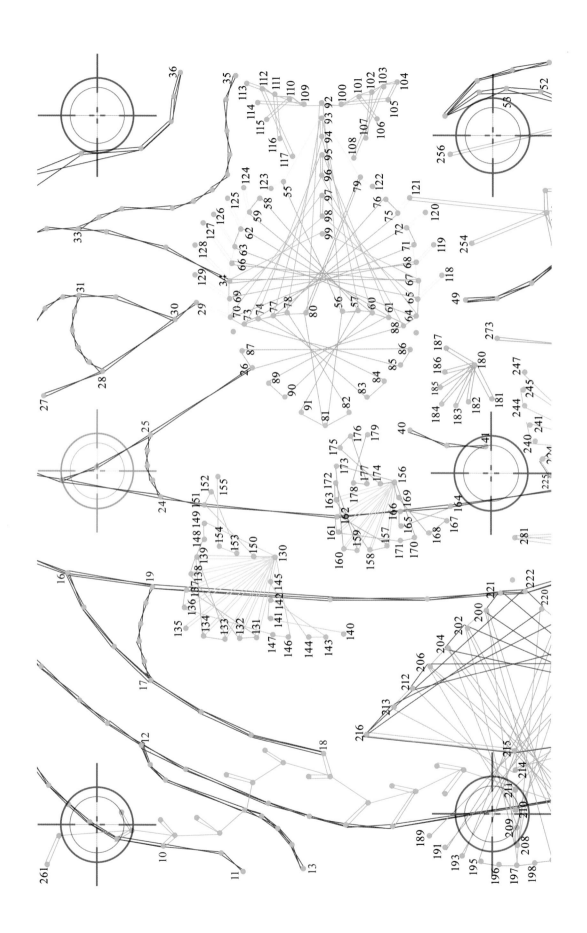

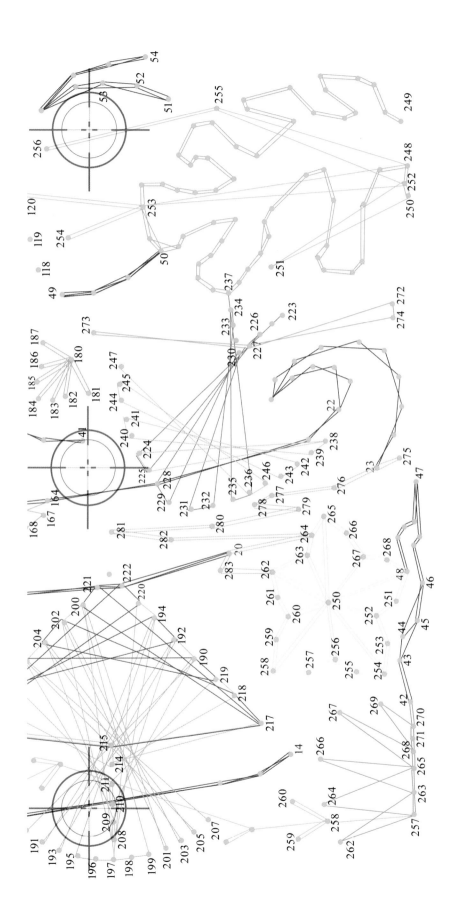

Vanishing Cheshire Cat

page 49

(enlarge 110%)

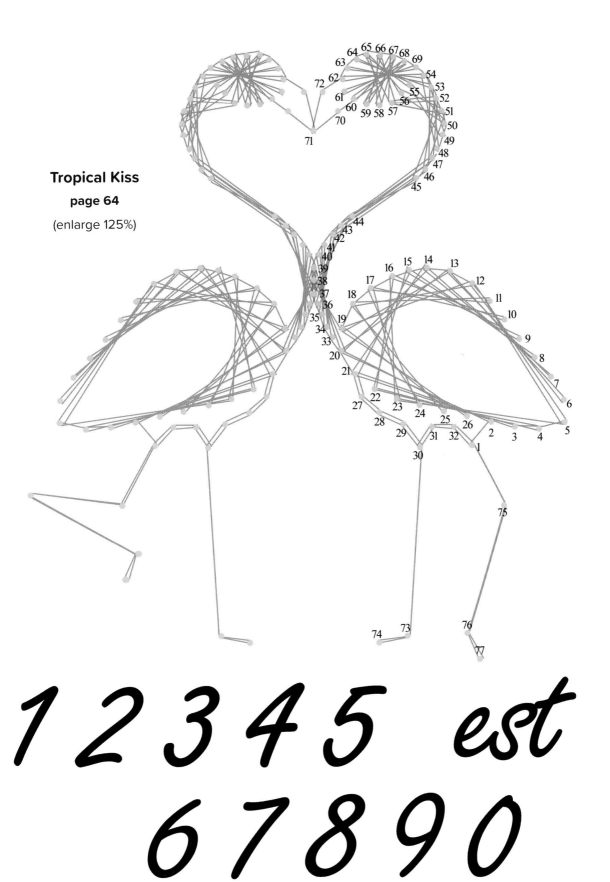

Tropical Kiss
page 64
(enlarge 125%)

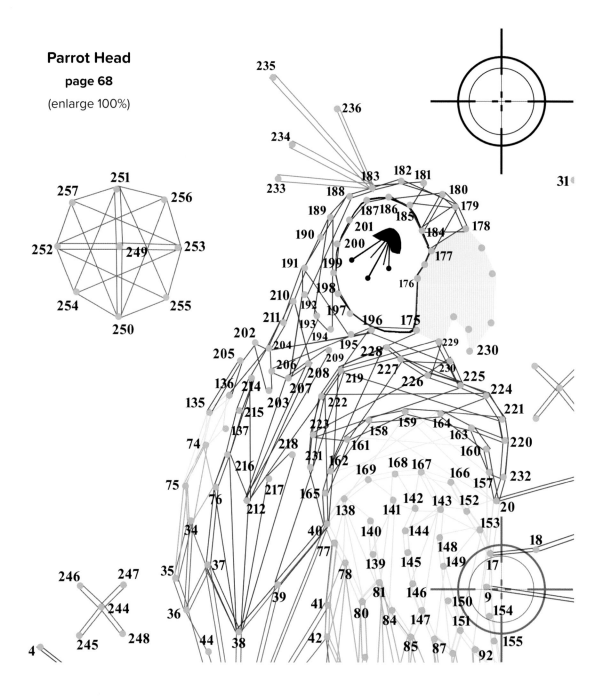

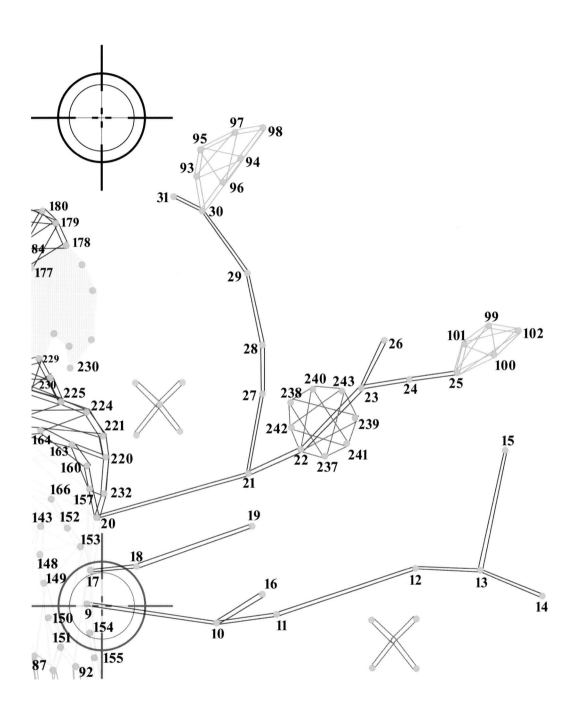

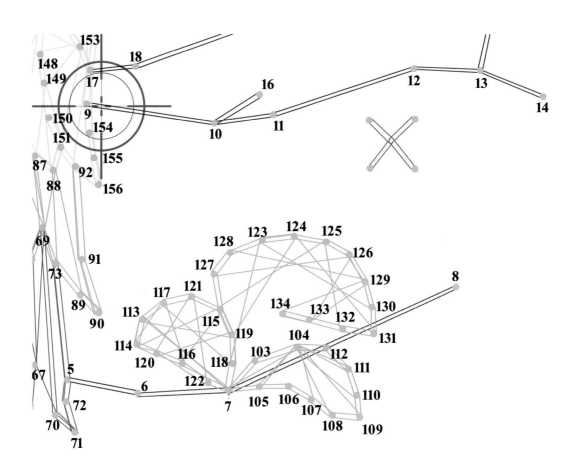
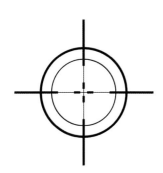

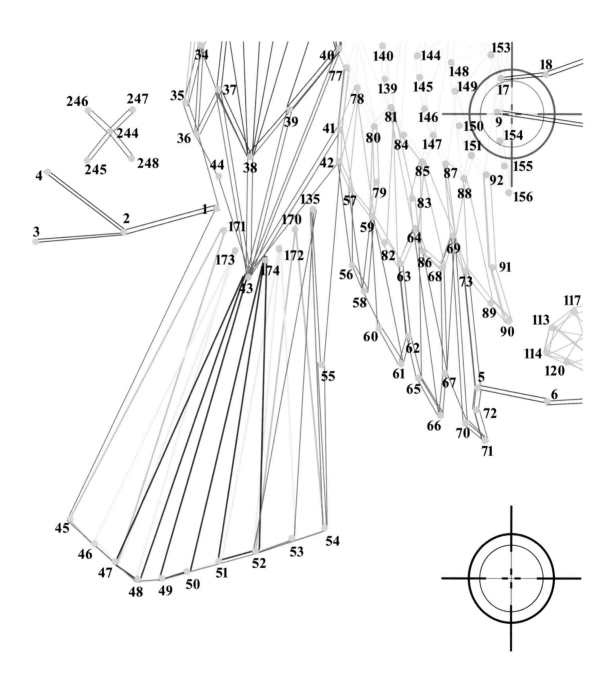

Geometric Letters

(enlarge 100%)

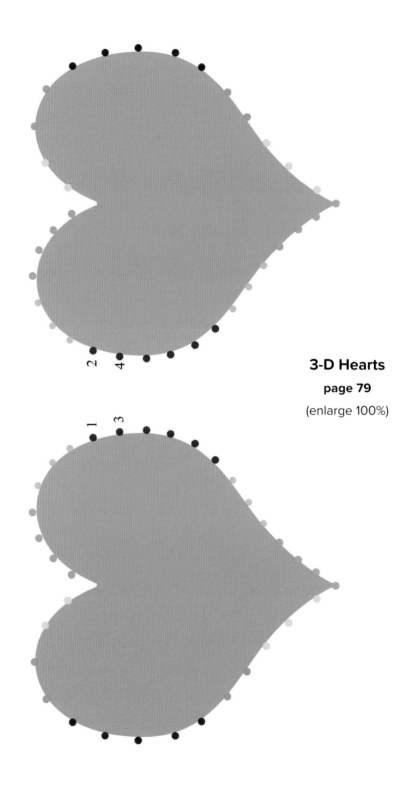

3-D Hearts

page 79

(enlarge 100%)

EXTRA PATTERNS

Chinese Dragon

(enlarge 154%)

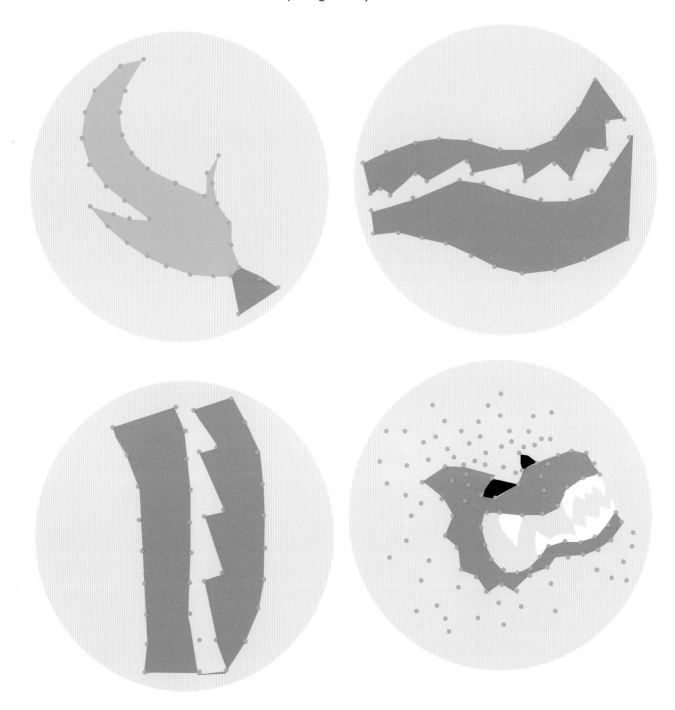

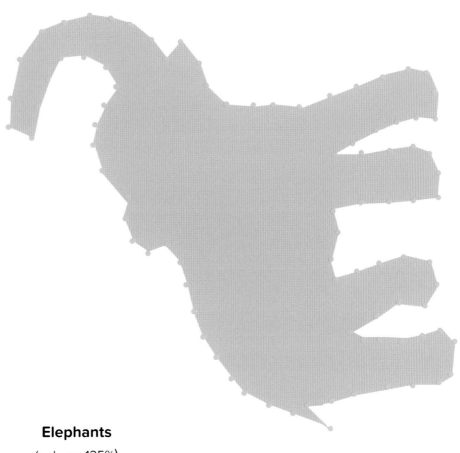

Elephants

(enlarge 125%)

Mushrooms

(enlarge 110%)

Pop Valentine

(enlarge 125%)

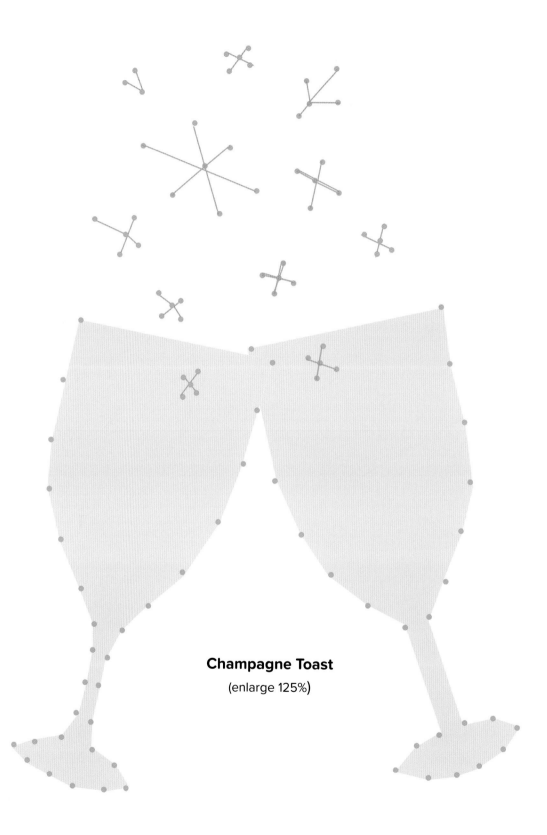

Champagne Toast

(enlarge 125%)

Zodiac Mandala

(enlarge 125%)

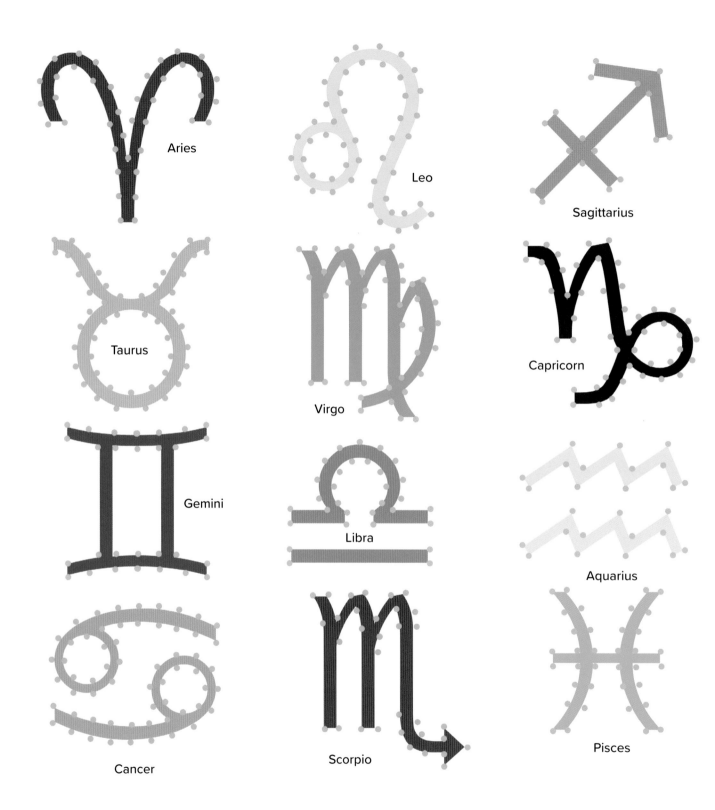

Aries

Leo

Sagittarius

Taurus

Virgo

Capricorn

Gemini

Libra

Aquarius

Cancer

Scorpio

Pisces

Note: Choose your desired zodiac sign from the pattern bank and swap it into the mandala circle (enlarge 154%)

Summer Tree

(enlarge 125%)

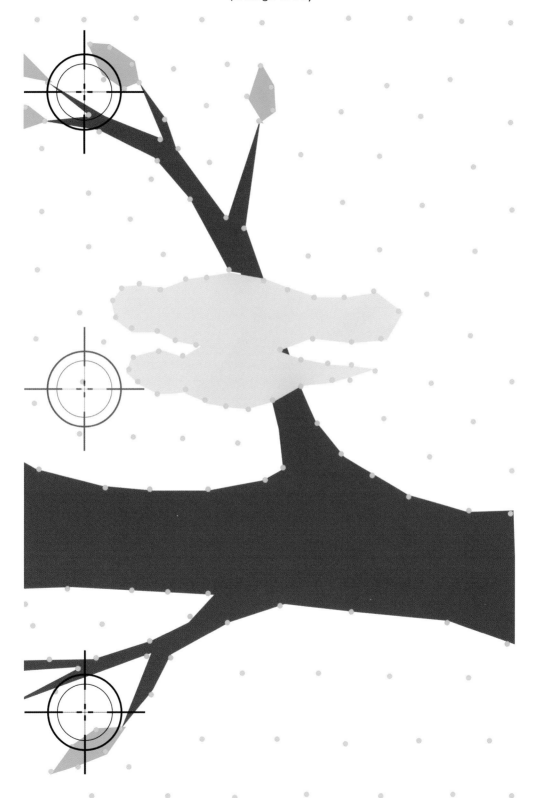

INDEX

Italicized text indicates a project.

PROJECT INDEX

ABOUT THE AUTHOR

Rain Blanken recently transplanted from the cornfield and airfields of Dayton, Ohio, to the Sunshine City of St. Petersburg, Florida. She is a senior editor at *The Penny Hoarder*, former host of About.com's *DIY Fashion*, and author of *The Complete Guide to Customizing Your Clothes* (2012). Rain is an avid peanut butter consumer, prefers Data over most robots, and if she were an action figure, she would come with her dog, Gizmo. Between smatterings of sunblock, this redhead enjoys days at the beach with her husband and three children.

MORE GREAT BOOKS *from*
SPRING HOUSE PRESS

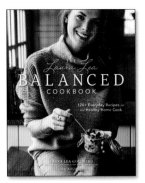

**The Laura Lea
Balanced Cookbook**
978-1940611-56-3
$35.00 | 368 Pages

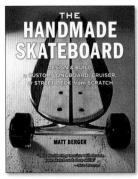

The Handmade Skateboard
978-1-940611-06-8
$24.95 | 160 Pages

Little Everyday Cakes
978-1-940611-67-9
$22.95 | 160 Pages

The Natural Beauty Solution
978-1-940611-18-1
$19.95 | 128 Pages

The Reclaimed Woodworker
978-1-940611-54-9
$24.95 | 176 pages

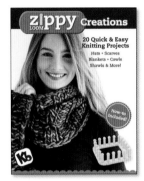

Zippy Loom Creations
978-1-940611-79-2
$16.99 | 88 Pages

Emoji Crochet
978-1-940611-72-3
$19.95 | 128 Pages

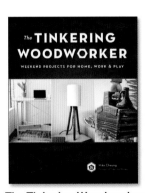

The Tinkering Woodworker
978-1-940611-08-2
$24.95 | 152 Pages

**Rock Art: A Gig Poster
Coloring Book**
978-1940611-42-6
$12.99 | 80 Pages

SPRING HOUSE PRESS

Look for these Spring House Press titles at your favorite bookstore, specialty retailer, or visit *www.springhousepress.com*.
For more information about Spring House Press, email us at *info@springhousepress.com*.